Beg.
Whole Fish
× Sauces/Mar.   Coriander Mayo P☺

P26 BBQ Fish × Coriander

29   BBQ Fish + Ginger + hime

32   Salmon × Ginger

35   Fish Gratins

38   Salmon × Salsa

Kebabs   P58 +

   Coconut Dalsa P65 with Prawn × Monkfish
   Turmeric Prawn P67 + Pineapple.
         Kebabs   71   Tuna Fish Saké
         Prawn   P78 Guacamole
         Prawn   P83 Spanish style
         Prawn   £89 Mango Dalsa
Angels on Horseback P93 with (sub) scallops (bacon)

Grill It!
Seafood

Grill It! Seafood

**80 Quick and Delicious Recipes
to Sear, Sizzle, and Smoke**

Edited by Anne McDowall

SALAMANDER

A Salamander Book

Published by Salamander Books Ltd.
8 Blenheim Court
Brewery Road
London N7 9NY
United Kingdom

© Salamander Books Ltd., 2003

A member of **Chrysalis** Books plc

ISBN 1 84065 451 1

1 3 5 7 9 8 6 4 2

Credits

Editor: Anne McDowall
Project Manager: Katherine Edelston
Designer: Cara Hamilton
Production: Ian Hughes
Colour reproduction: Anorax Imaging Ltd.
Printed in China

The recipes in this book have appeared in previous Salamander titles by other authors and have been edited by Anne McDowall for this edition.

Notes

All spoon measurements are level: 1 teaspoon = 5ml spoon; 1 tablespoon = 15ml spoon
Cooking times given are approximate: they will vary according to the starting temperature of the food and its thickness as well as the heat of the barbecue.
All recipes in this book assume that fish has been cleaned and scaled.

Contents

Introduction

What better way to cook all sorts of fish than on a barbecue – it's quick, it's healthy and the fish not only retains all its natural flavour, but can also be enhanced by wonderfully exotic spices in marinades, glazes and accompanying dips and sauces. As with any barbecuing, there are a few things you need to know – for food to taste its best and to be safe – but barbecues are basically fun, social occasions, so relax and experiment!

Choosing a barbecue

There is a variety of different types of barbecue available, so if you are just starting out, or want to replace your existing model, it's worth taking some time to think about the various options to decide which would suit you best.

Although the traditional barbecue burns charcoal (or wood), there's a lot to be said for a gas or electric alternative. Neither requires starter fuel and both retain heat evenly. Gas barbecues, in particular, ignite almost instantaneously (electric types take about 10 minutes to heat) and can be used at any time of year. Their main disadvantage is the cumbersome gas bottle, which all models require. Although, of course, electric barbecues must not be used in the rain, the more sophisticated models can be used indoors with suitable ducting.

Purists will argue that the fun of barbecues is cooking over a real fire. Another big advantage of charcoal-burning models is their cost: a basic model will be cheaper than its gas or electric counterpart. Although you have the ongoing cost of fuel, neither

Barbecue accessories

As well as the barbecue, suitable fuel and firelighters, there are a number of other tools and accessories that are worth considering. Some are virtually indispensable; others will be very useful for cooking particular foods.

- Wooden block or table – for keeping implements and tools close at hand.
- Wire baskets – rectangular hinged meshes and fish-shaped ones are ideal for holding delicate fish that are being cooked directly on the barbecue and enable them to be turned easily.
- Skewers – square metal, long wooden or bamboo. The latter need to be soaked for about 20 minutes before use.

- Tongs and forks – ones with long handles are essential to keep hands away from heat source.
- Metal griddle plate – for cooking certain fragile foods on.
- Brushes – for basting food while it is cooking.
- Heavy-duty aluminium foil – for wrapping food to be cooked on the barbecue.
- Battery-operated fan – useful for fanning coals.
- Apron – a thick one with pockets is ideal.
- Oven gloves – but avoid the double-handed types.
- Water sprayer – for dousing unruly flames.
- Stiff wire brush and metal scrapers – for cleaning the barbecue.

lumpwood charcoal nor pressed briquettes (the most popular fuel types) are very expensive. Of the two, the former is the cheaper, lights more easily and burns hotter, but pressed briquettes burn for longer once alight. You can also buy aromatic wood chips to place on the ashen coals, which will impart wonderful, subtle flavours to the food.

Assuming you don't go for a disposable barbecue – basically a tin tray containing charcoal – the simplest option is a shallow metal bowl on a frame. There is no venting or cover but it is easy to light and simple to control. Better still is a kettle barbecue with its own hood, which will be suitable for all types of barbecuing – the hood will help protect food in bad weather, prevent spattering and billowing of smoke, and will also enable you to smoke food.

Always go for a larger model than you think you might need – even if you only cook small amounts of food, this will allow you to move the food around, to hotter or cooler areas as necessary.

Safety checklist
- Position the barbecue carefully on even ground and away from trees and fences.
- Never use lighter fluid, paraffin or petrol to light a barbecue.
- Avoid using an electric grill in wet weather.
- Never leave a lit barbecue unattended and be particularly vigilant with children.
- Keep a water spray handy to douse flames if they become unruly.
- Use long-handled tools to keep hands away from flames and avoid double-handed oven gloves, which can easily catch in the flames.
- Allow a transportable barbecue to cool completely before packing it away.
- Hot embers take several hours to cool: make sure they are cold before disposing of them.

Cooking on the barbecue

Before you light the barbecue, ensure it is in the right position, as a lit barbecue will be heavy – and possibly unsafe – to move. Spread a single layer of coals over the base, pile them up a little in the centre and push in firelighters or jelly starters. (Follow the manufacturer's instructions carefully if you are using ignition fluid and never use petrol, paraffin or other similar flammable liquids.) Light with a taper and, as soon as the fire has caught, spread out coals and add a few more. The barbecue is ready to start cooking on only when the flames have died down and the charcoal is covered with white ash – this will usually take at least half an hour. Charcoal will burn for about an hour and a half and you can add other pieces around the edges occasionally.

Although it is easy to adjust the heat on gas and electric barbecues, it is more difficult on an open-grid type unless you have a kettle barbecue with adjustable vents. If the coals have become too hot, either place the food away from the centre of the barbecue or push coals aside to distribute their heat. To make the fire hotter, poke away the ash, push coals together and gently blow (or use a battery-operated fan). To test the temperature of the barbecue, place your open hand carefully over the coals: if you can keep it there for as long as 5 seconds, the temperature is low; 3-4 seconds it is medium hot, and for 2 seconds it is hot. The right height for cooking is about 5-7.5cm (2-3in) above the grid. On a lidded barbecue, the heat will be greater when the lid is lowered.

When you have finished cooking, spread out the coals so that they cool faster. Cleaning the grill rack is best done while still hot: use a metal scraper to dislodge bits of food into the fire. If necessary, you can wash the grill rack with soapy water once it has cooled. When the embers are completely cold (this will take several hours), sift away surplus ash and cover the barbecue for future use.

Choosing fish

Really fresh fish looks bright with vivid markings. The eyes are clear, bright and slightly protruding and the gills pinkish or bright red. Skin is firm and bright with bright scales that adhere tightly. The flesh is firm and elastic and springs back when pressed. Any smell is fresh and clean with a hint of the sea (exceptions are shark and skate, which give off a natural smell of ammonia, which disappears on cooking). Fillets and steaks should feel firm, not dry or shrivelled, and cut surfaces look translucent. Avoid any that look slimy or have brown or yellow patches at the edges. If packaged, there should not be any milky liquid.

A lot of the fish sold in supermarkets, and some fishmongers, is thawed frozen fish. This has an unfortunate toll on its quality and limits its life. Thawed frozen fish should not be refrozen.

Substitutions

As fish and seafood are regional and seasonal, you may not be able to buy the type specified in a recipe, but substitutions are often possible, especially for fillets or steaks. Below are some examples:

Plaice / whiting / flounder
Sole / brill / plaice / flounder
Brill / turbot / John Dory
Bream / John Dory
Cod / haddock / halibut / hake / monkfish
Red snapper / grouper / mahi mahi / bream
Pompano / pomfret / bream
Red mullet / bream / snapper
Tuna / swordfish
Mackerel / herring
Bass / salmon (especially steaks and fillets)

Preparing and cooking fish

The recipes in this book assume that fish has been cleaned and scaled; a fishmonger will do this for you. Skinning round fish presents no problems, but skinning flat fish, such as plaice, is more difficult and you may prefer to get your fishmonger to do it for you. Filleting is quick and easy after a little practice and providing you use a filleting knife. This has a flexible, pointed, straight-edged blade about 15cm (6in) long. With this type of knife you can feel round soft fish bones, removing every last scrap of flesh from them. A really sharp edge to the blade is vital for skinning, boning or filleting fish quickly, easily and efficiently. However fish skin will blunt the edge of the knife quickly, so it will need frequent sharpening. You will also need a heavy knife for removing fish heads, kitchen scissors for snipping away fins, a large board and a clean damp cloth. Handle skinned and filleted fish with care and cook as soon as possible. You can keep trimmings to use for stock.

Using marinades Marinades are often used with foods that are to be barbecued: not only does oil in a marinade help prevent food from sticking, but added herbs and spices create mouthwatering flavours. Fish and shellfish generally require a shorter marinating time than meat. If food has been marinated in the refrigerator, allow it to come back to room temperature before cooking.

Grilling Many types of fish are suitable for barbecuing directly on top of the flame, but delicate varieties are best contained in a hinged wire basket.

Cooking in foil Delicate fish can also be wrapped in heavy-duty or double-thickness aluminium foil. Wrapping fish also helps to prevent the outside of the food from burning before the inside is cooked and keeps juices trapped inside.

Pan-frying You can use a griddle or heavy-based frying pan on the barbecue in the same way as on a conventional cooker hob and this is a good way to cook fish. Grease the surface and make sure the coals are very hot for a successful result.

Using skewers Firm fish, such as tuna, swordfish or monkfish, is the best to use for kebabs. And, of course, seafood, such as prawns, is delicious cooked this way too. Most skewered food is marinated first. Bamboo skewers need soaking before use and metal ones should be oiled.

Smoking To dry smoke, no water bath is needed and this is generally the method used for fish. The fish should first be soaked in salted water and then left out on a rack to dry completely, after which it is cooked in a closed, or foil-tented barbecue over low coals for a long time.

Skinning flat fish (1)

Flat fish are usually skinned before filleting. Lay the fish dark side uppermost and head away from you. Make an incision in the skin across the bone where the tail joins the body. Working from the cut, loosen a flap of skin with a thumbnail or knife. Hold the tail firmly with one hand (a cloth or a little salt on your fingertips will help you to grip it) and pull the skin backwards towards the head, not up. When you have removed the skin as far as the jaws, turn the fish over and, holding it by the head, pull the skin until you reach the tail.

Filleting flat fish (2)

Place the fish with its head away from you, eyes facing up. With the point of a knife, slit along the backbone from head to tail. Insert the knife blade between the flesh and ribs to one side of the back-bone, next to the head. With short, slicing movements, keeping the blade next to the ribs at a shallow angle, separate flesh from bones. Cut the fillet off at the tail and trim. Remove the other fillet on top of the bone, then turn the fish over and repeat.

Filleting round fish (3)

Round fish are usually skinned after filleting: you will get two fillets. Place the fish on its side and place the point of the knife beside the dorsal fin. Cut down along the backbone to the tail, keeping the blade just above the centre of the backbone, but close to the upper bones of the rib cage. Cut from the dorsal fin to the head. Raise the top fillet slightly and, working from head to tail, work the fillet away from the ribs with a slicing motion of the blade. Slice along the backbone again, this time with the knife placed just below the centre. Lift away the backbone and ribs from the fish.

Skinning fillets (4)

Lay the fillet skin side down on a work surface and make an incision through the flesh across the tail end. With the knife blade, loosen about 1cm (½in) of flesh. Grip the skin at the tail end (a little salt on your fingertips or a cloth will help you to grip it), slant the knife away from you and work towards the head, slicing through the flesh, close to skin, and pushing flesh away with the knife.

Whole Fish

Grilled Plaice with Hot Sauce

SERVES 2

1 PLAICE, WEIGHING ABOUT
575G (1½LB)

SALT AND FRESHLY GROUND BLACK PEPPER

1 TABLESPOON VEGETABLE OIL,
PLUS EXTRA FOR BRUSHING

½ TEASPOON MINCED GARLIC

½ TEASPOON CHOPPED FRESH GINGER

2 SHALLOTS, FINELY CHOPPED

2-3 SMALL FRESH RED CHILLIES,
SEEDED AND CHOPPED

1 TABLESPOON CHOPPED SPRING ONION

2 TABLESPOONS FISH SAUCE

1 TEASPOON SUGAR

1 TABLESPOON TAMARIND WATER
OR LIME JUICE

2-3 TABLESPOONS CHICKEN STOCK
OR WATER

2 TEASPOONS CORNFLOUR

◆ Score both sides of fish at 2.5cm (1in) intervals and rub with salt and pepper. Leave to stand for 25 minutes.

◆ Brush both sides of fish with oil and place on the rack over hot coals. Cook for about 4 minutes on each side until lightly brown but not burnt. Place on a warmed serving dish.

◆ Heat 1 tablespoon oil in a small pan and stir-fry garlic, ginger, shallots, chillies and spring onion for 1 minute.

◆ Add fish sauce, sugar, tamarind water or lime juice and stock or water. Bring to the boil and simmer for 30 seconds.

◆ Mix cornflour with 1 tablespoon water and stir into sauce to thicken. Pour sauce over fish and serve.

Malaysian-style Plaice

SERVES 4

*4 PLAICE, EACH WEIGHING ABOUT
350G (12OZ)*

*4 LARGE GARLIC CLOVES,
CUT INTO FINE SLIVERS*

*2.5CM (1IN) PIECE FRESH GINGER,
CUT INTO FINE SLIVERS*

4 TABLESPOONS GROUNDNUT OIL

4 TABLESPOONS LIGHT SOY SAUCE

1 TABLESPOON SESAME OIL

1 TABLESPOON RICE WINE

4 SPRING ONIONS, THINLY SLICED

◆ With the point of a sharp knife, cut 5 diagonal slashes, herringbone style, in both sides of each fish. Place fish in a shallow dish.

◆ Put garlic, ginger, groundnut oil, soy sauce, sesame oil and rice wine in a small saucepan. Heat to simmering point and pour over fish, spooning marinade into slashes. Refrigerate for at least 1 hour, turning fish every 30 minutes.

◆ Lift fish from marinade and place on the rack of a prepared barbecue, preferably in rectangular, hinged wire baskets, pale skin side down. Cook for about 2 minutes. Turn carefully and cook for an additional 2 or 3 minutes depending on thickness of fish.

◆ Reheat any remaining marinade and pour over fish. Scatter over spring onions and serve.

Tandoori Trout

SERVES 2

Seeds from 6 cardamom pods

2 teaspoons cumin seeds

4 tablespoons Greek-style yogurt

1 large garlic clove, chopped

2 tablespoons lime juice

2.5cm (1in) piece fresh ginger, chopped

1 teaspoon garam masala

Pinch ground turmeric

¼ teaspoon cayenne

Salt

1 teaspoon red food colouring (optional)

2 trout, each weighing about 300g (10oz)

Vegetable oil for brushing

Rice with chillies and tomato and onion salad, to serve (optional)

Lemon and lime wedges and coriander sprigs, to garnish (optional)

◆ Heat a small, heavy pan. Add cardamom and cumin seeds and heat until fragrant. Place seeds in a mortar or small bowl and crush with a pestle or the end of a rolling pin.

◆ Place yogurt, garlic, lime juice, ginger, garam masala, turmeric, cayenne and salt into a blender or small food processor and mix together to make a paste. Add food colouring, if using.

◆ With the point of a sharp knife, make 3 deep slashes in each side of each trout. Spread spice mixture over trout, working it into slashes.

◆ Place trout into a shallow, nonmetallic dish in a single layer. Cover and leave to marinate in refrigerator for 4 hours.

◆ Sprinkle a little oil over fish, place on the rack of a prepared barbecue and cook for about 7 minutes on each side.

◆ Serve with chilli rice and tomato and onion salad, garnished with lemon and lime wedges and coriander sprigs, if desired.

Baked Trout with Thai Spices

SERVES 4

4 MEDIUM TROUT

OIL FOR BRUSHING

RED CURRY PASTE

8 DRIED RED CHILLIES, SEEDED AND CHOPPED

8 CORIANDER ROOTS, WASHED AND CHOPPED

1 TABLESPOON GRATED FRESH GINGER

2 LEMON GRASS STALKS, CHOPPED

4 KAFFIR LIME LEAVES, SHREDDED, OR GRATED ZEST 2 LIMES

4 GARLIC CLOVES, CHOPPED

2 SHALLOTS, CHOPPED

SALT AND 1 TEASPOON GROUND BLACK PEPPER

SAUCE

1 BUNCH SPRING ONIONS, CHOPPED

4 TABLESPOONS DARK SOY SAUCE

4 TABLESPOONS DRY SHERRY

JUICE 2 LIMES

2 TABLESPOONS CHOPPED FRESH CORIANDER

◆ Wash and dry trout and cut 4 slashes in each side.

◆ To make curry paste, place dried chillies, coriander roots, ginger, lemon grass, lime leaves, garlic, shallots and salt and pepper in a blender and purée until smooth. Spread mixture all over inside and outside of trout.

◆ Lightly oil 4 sheets of aluminium foil and place a trout in the centre of each one. Draw up edges of foil, leaving a gap at the top.

◆ To make sauce, combine spring onions, soy sauce, sherry, 4 tablespoons water, lime juice and chopped coriander in a bowl. Divide sauce between packages.

◆ Seal package edges by twisting foil then place on the rack of a prepared barbecue and cook for 20-25 minutes until trout are cooked through. Serve at once.

Red Mullet with Fennel

6 RED MULLET, EACH WEIGHING ABOUT
175G (6OZ)

2 SMALL FENNEL BULBS, THICKLY SLICED

300ML (10FL OZ) OLIVE OIL

85ML (3FL OZ) DRY WHITE WINE

1 GARLIC CLOVE, ROUGHLY CHOPPED

1 SMALL RED CHILLI, SEEDED AND SLICED

4 THYME SPRIGS, BRUISED

2 PARSLEY SPRIGS, BRUISED

1 TEASPOON CORIANDER SEEDS, CRUSHED

½ TEASPOON FENNEL SEEDS

SALT AND PEPPER

◆ Wash mullet inside and out and dry well. Cut 2 small slashes through the skin of each fish on both sides, and place in a large, shallow dish. Add fennel slices.

◆ Mix together olive oil, wine, garlic, chilli, thyme, parsley, coriander and fennel seeds and salt and pepper. Pour over fish, cover and leave to marinate for several hours or overnight, turning fish and fennel in marinade occasionally.

◆ Remove fish and fennel from marinade. Barbecue fish for 4-5 minutes on each side and fennel for 2-3 minutes on each side until both are cooked and lightly charred. Baste with marinade if necessary.

◆ Serve immediately, with crusty bread and a crisp green salad if desired.

Smoked Bream

SERVES 4-6

2 BREAM, EACH WEIGHING ABOUT
450-700G (1-1½LB)

115G (4OZ) SEA SALT

2 HANDFULS HICKORY CHIPS

OLIVE OIL

◆ Put bream in a large shallow glass or plastic dish. Dissolve salt in 1 litre (1¾ pints) cold water. Pour over fish and leave to soak for at least 30 minutes.

◆ Drain fish thoroughly. Put on wire rack and leave in an airy room for about 2½ hours until dry. Fish must be dry to touch before being smoked. Meanwhile, soak hickory chips in water for 30 minutes.

◆ Using a covered barbecue, light coals and push to one side (fish must not be placed directly over coals). Wait until burned down to white ash stage, then add drained hickory chips.

◆ Thoroughly brush each fish with oil and place on the barbecue rack away from coals. Close lid and barbecue fish for 30-45 minutes, turning once, or until flesh flakes when tested with a knife.

Variation: Use red snapper instead of bream, if preferred.

Mullet with Anchovy Sauce

4 RED MULLET, EACH WEIGHING ABOUT 225G (8OZ)

4 CANNED ANCHOVY FILLETS, RINSED AND CUT INTO 4 PIECES EACH

FLOUR FOR COATING

OIL FOR BRUSHING

SALT AND FRESHLY GROUND BLACK PEPPER

CHOPPED FRESH PARSLEY, CAPERS AND 1 ORANGE, PEELED AND DIVIDED INTO SEGMENTS, TO GARNISH

ANCHOVY SAUCE

115ML (4FL OZ) FRESHLY SQUEEZED ORANGE JUICE

4 TABLESPOONS SKINNED, SEEDED AND CHOPPED TOMATO

4 CANNED ANCHOVY FILLETS, RINSED AND ROUGHLY CHOPPED

PEPPER, TO TASTE

◆ Using the point of a sharp knife, cut 2 diagonal slashes in both sides of each fish. Insert a piece of anchovy fillet in each slash.

◆ Season flour with salt and pepper, then coat fish lightly and evenly. Brush fish with oil.

◆ Place fish on a rack over hot coals and cook until crisp, about 5 minutes each side. Transfer to a serving plate and keep warm.

◆ To make sauce, put orange juice, tomato, anchovies and pepper into a pan. Boil gently until thickened to a light sauce. Add water if necessary.

◆ Serve fish with sauce and garnish with parsley, capers and orange segments.

Barbecued Grey Mullet

SERVES 6

1 grey mullet, weighing about 1.5kg (3½lb)

Salt and freshly ground black pepper

1 bay leaf

1 rosemary sprig

85ml (3fl oz) olive oil

Juice 2 small lemons

1 teaspoon dried oregano

1 tablespoon chopped fresh parsley

2 garlic cloves, finely chopped

Bay leaves and lemon wedges, to serve

◆ Season cavity of fish with salt and pepper. Place bay leaf and rosemary inside fish.

◆ Place mullet on the rack of a prepared barbecue over medium coals and cook for about 10 minutes on each side.

◆ In a bowl, whisk together olive oil, lemon juice, oregano, parsley and garlic until thick.

◆ Lay fish on a serving platter and garnish with bay leaves and lemon wedges. Pour sauce over fish and serve at once.

Spiced Sweet and Sour Fish

1 TABLESPOON CUMIN SEEDS

1 TEASPOON CORIANDER SEEDS

3 TABLESPOONS VEGETABLE OIL

½ FRESH RED CHILLI, SEEDED AND FINELY CHOPPED

3 GARLIC CLOVES, SMASHED

2 ONIONS, CHOPPED

2.5CM (1IN) PIECE SHRIMP PASTE, ROASTED (SEE NOTE)

3½ TABLESPOONS LIME JUICE

3 TABLESPOONS DARK SOY SAUCE

BROWN SUGAR, TO TASTE

2 WHOLE FISH, EACH WEIGHING ABOUT 700G (1½LB)

◆ Heat cumin and coriander seeds in a frying pan over medium-high heat until toasted with a fragrant roasted aroma. Cool slightly then grind in a small blender or using a pestle and mortar.

◆ Heat oil in a small frying pan over medium-high heat. Add chilli, garlic and onions and fry until lightly browned. Tip into blender containing cumin and coriander.

◆ Add shrimp paste, lime juice and soy sauce and mix to a thin paste. Add 115ml (4fl oz) hot water, and brown sugar to taste. Set aside.

◆ Cut 3 deep slashes on both sides of each fish and score along backbone. Place on the rack of a prepared barbecue.

◆ Cook for about 6-7 minutes on each side. Flesh should just flake when tested with the point of a sharp knife, and skin should be brown.

◆ Reheat sauce, pour some over fish and serve remainder separately.

Note: To roast shrimp paste, hold it in tongs over a naked flame, turning it so it roasts evenly.

Trout in Vine Leaves

SERVES 4

4 TROUT

2 TABLESPOONS OLIVE OIL

GRATED ZEST 1 SEVILLE ORANGE

2 TABLESPOONS FRESHLY SQUEEZED ORANGE JUICE

1 GARLIC CLOVE, CRUSHED

SEEDS FROM 6 CARDAMOM PODS, CRUSHED

½ TEASPOON SALT

½ TEASPOON BLACK PEPPER

1 TEASPOON DIJON MUSTARD

2 BAY LEAVES

3 TEASPOONS CHOPPED FENNEL

8 VINE LEAVES

1 TEASPOON ARROWROOT

FENNEL SPRIGS AND BAY LEAVES, TO GARNISH

◆ Rinse fish under running water and dry on absorbent kitchen paper. Score flesh on each side.

◆ To make marinade, mix together olive oil, orange zest and juice, garlic, cardamom seeds, salt, pepper, mustard, bay leaves and fennel.

◆ Immerse fish in marinade and turn to coat evenly. Cover with cling film and leave in a cool place to marinate for 1 hour.

◆ Take fish out of marinade, reserving marinade, and loosely wrap each fish in 2 vine leaves.

◆ Arrange fish on the rack of a preheated barbecue and cook for about 6 minutes on each side. Unwrap fish and arrange on individual plates.

◆ Blend remaining marinade with arrowroot. Put in a saucepan and bring to the boil, stirring. Cook for 1 minute, until thickened and glossy.

◆ Pour sauce over fish and garnish with fennel sprigs and bay leaves.

Variation: Use 8 small red mullet instead of trout.

Bass with Fennel

SERVES 6

1 BASS OR BREAM, WEIGHING ABOUT 3KG (6¾LB)

1 BUNCH FENNEL

SALT AND FRESHLY GROUND BLACK PEPPER

JUICE 1 LEMON

3 TABLESPOONS OLIVE OIL

LIME SLICES AND FENNEL SPRIGS, TO GARNISH

◆ With a sharp knife, cut deep diagonal slashes in each side of fish and insert a fennel sprig into each slash. Season fish inside and out with salt and pepper and put 2-3 fennel sprigs in cavity.

◆ Mix together lemon juice and oil. Brush over top half of fish and sprinkle a little inside fish.

◆ Place fish on the preheated barbecue rack, brushed side down, and lay a fennel sprig on top. Cook for 10-12 minutes until bottom half is cooked and skin is lightly charred.

◆ Turn over fish carefully, brush with lemon juice and oil and place another fennel sprig on top. Cook for a further 10-12 minutes, until cooked through.

◆ Cut into portions, garnish with lime slices and fennel sprigs and serve.

Fillets and Steaks

Brill with Wild Mushroom Sauce

SERVES 4

2 TABLESPOONS DRIED PORCINI MUSHROOMS

4 TABLESPOONS BRANDY

150ML (5FL OZ) VEGETABLE STOCK

4 TABLESPOONS OLIVE OIL

2 SHALLOTS, CHOPPED

225G (8OZ) MIXED WILD MUSHROOMS (E.G. CHANTERELLES, PORCINI, BLEWITS, OYSTER), CHOPPED IF LARGE

4 BRILL FILLETS

55G (2OZ) UNSALTED BUTTER, SOFTENED

SALT AND PEPPER

1 TABLESPOON CHOPPED FRESH PARSLEY

◆ Soak dried porcini mushrooms in 150ml (5fl oz) boiling water for 30 minutes. Strain, reserving liquid, and chop.

◆ Place reserved mushroom stock, brandy and vegetable stock in a pan. Bring to the boil, reduce heat and simmer to reduce until only about 150ml (5fl oz) remains. Set aside.

◆ In a pan, fry shallots in 2 tablespoons olive oil for 3 minutes. Add fresh and soaked mushrooms and stir-fry for 5 minutes. Cover and keep warm.

◆ Brush fish fillets with remaining oil and place on the rack of a prepared barbecue for about 2-3 minutes on each side until cooked.

◆ Meanwhile, bring reduced stock to a rolling boil. Whisk in butter, a little at a time, until sauce is thickened and glossy. Season to taste.

◆ Transfer fish to warmed plates, spoon over mushrooms and pour over sauce. Sprinkle with parsley and serve at once.

Fillet of Turbot with Braised Leeks

SERVES 4

25G (1OZ) BUTTER

2 SHALLOTS, QUARTERED

2 TEASPOONS YELLOW MUSTARD SEEDS

450G (1LB) BABY LEEKS, CUT INTO THIN SLICES

4 TABLESPOONS DRY SHERRY

2 TABLESPOONS CHOPPED FRESH CHERVIL

SALT AND PEPPER

4 SMALL TURBOT FILLETS

1 TABLESPOON OLIVE OIL

BABY POTATOES AND CARROTS, TO SERVE (OPTIONAL)

◆ Melt butter in a pan, add shallots and mustard seeds and fry for 3 minutes. Add leeks and fry for a further 3 minutes.

◆ Add sherry, cover and cook over a low heat for 5-8 minutes until leeks are tender. Stir in chervil and season to taste.

◆ Meanwhile, wash turbot fillets and pat dry. Brush with a little oil and place on the rack of a prepared barbecue for 3-4 minutes on each side until cooked through.

◆ Serve turbot on a bed of braised leeks, with baby potatoes and carrots, if desired.

Note: Turbot is an expensive fish and may be difficult to find, but its delicate flavour works well with leeks. Plaice makes a good substitute.

Barbecued Fish with Coriander

SERVES 4

700G (1½LB) GREY MULLET OR
MONKFISH FILLETS

3 TABLESPOONS OLIVE OIL

2 GARLIC CLOVES, CRUSHED

2 TEASPOONS CUMIN SEEDS,
TOASTED AND GROUND

1 TEASPOON PAPRIKA

1 FRESH GREEN CHILLI, SEEDED AND
FINELY CHOPPED

HANDFUL CORIANDER LEAVES,
FINELY CHOPPED

3 TABLESPOONS LIME JUICE

SALT

HOT COOKED RICE, TO SERVE (OPTIONAL)

MINT SPRIGS AND LIME WEDGES,
TO GARNISH

◆ Place fish into a shallow nonmetallic dish. In a bowl mix together olive oil, garlic, cumin, paprika, chilli, coriander, lime juice and salt.

◆ Spoon marinade over fish. Cover and refrigerate for 3-4 hours, turning fish in marinade occasionally.

◆ Remove fish from marinade and place on the rack of a prepared barbecue. Cook for about 4 minutes on each side, basting with coriander mixture occasionally, until flesh flakes when tested with the point of a sharp knife.

◆ Serve fish warm on a bed of rice, if desired, and garnish with mint sprigs and lime wedges.

Bass with Ginger and Lime

SERVES 6-8

2 SHALLOTS, FINELY CHOPPED

4CM (½IN) PIECE FRESH GINGER, FINELY CHOPPED

JUICE 2 LIMES

4 TABLESPOONS RICE WINE VINEGAR

250ML (9FL OZ) OLIVE OIL

2 TABLESPOONS CHINESE SESAME OIL

2 TABLESPOONS SOY SAUCE

SALT AND PEPPER

6-8 BASS FILLETS, EACH WEIGHING ABOUT 175G (6OZ) AND ABOUT 1CM (½IN) THICK

BUNCH FRESH CORIANDER

TOASTED SESAME SEEDS, TO GARNISH

◆ In a bowl mix together shallots, ginger, lime juice, rice wine vinegar, olive and sesame oils, soy sauce, salt and pepper.

◆ Brush fish lightly with ginger mixture and place on the rack of a prepared barbecue. Cook for 2-3 minutes on each side, basting occasionally with ginger mixture.

◆ Before serving, place remaining ginger mixture in a pan, bring to the boil, then remove from the heat.

◆ Chop coriander leaves and discard stalks. Reserve a few whole leaves for garnish. Mix chopped coriander into ginger mixture.

◆ Spoon some sauce onto serving plates, then place barbecued fish on top.

◆ Sprinkle with sesame seeds and garnish with coriander leaves to serve.

Sesame-coated Whiting

SERVES 4

1 tablespoon Dijon mustard

1 tablespoon tomato purée

*1½ teaspoons finely chopped
fresh tarragon*

Squeeze lemon juice

Pepper

70g (2½oz) sesame seeds

2 tablespoons plain flour

1 egg, lightly beaten

*4 whiting fillets, each weighing
about 150g (5oz), skinned*

Olive oil for brushing

*Tarragon sprigs and lemon wedges,
to garnish (optional)*

◆ In a small bowl mix together mustard, tomato purée, tarragon, lemon juice and pepper.

◆ Combine sesame seeds and flour and spread evenly on a large plate. Pour beaten egg into a shallow bowl.

◆ Spread mustard mixture over both sides of each fish fillet, then dip fillet in beaten egg. Coat fish evenly in sesame seeds and flour mixture, then refrigerate for 30 minutes.

◆ Place coated fillets on the rack of a prepared barbecue (ideally in hinged wire baskets). Brush one side of each fillet lightly with oil, then cook for 2-3 minutes. Turn fish over, lightly brush top with oil and cook for 2-3 minutes longer.

◆ Transfer fish to a warm serving plate to serve and garnish with lemon wedges and tarragon sprigs, if desired.

Cod with Teriyaki Glaze

2 TABLESPOONS SOY SAUCE

1 TABLESPOON RICE WINE OR
MEDIUM-DRY SHERRY

1 TABLESPOON LIGHT SOFT BROWN SUGAR

1 TEASPOON GRATED FRESH GINGER

4 COD FILLETS WITH SKIN

CHERVIL SPRIGS, TO GARNISH

STIR-FRIED VEGETABLES, TO SERVE
(OPTIONAL)

◆ To make teriyaki glaze, gently heat together soy sauce, rice wine or sherry, sugar and ginger for 2-3 minutes in a small saucepan until lightly syrupy. Leave to cool.

◆ Brush both sides of fish fillets with teriyaki glaze. Place on the rack of a preheated barbecue and cook for 3-4 minutes on each side.

◆ Transfer fish to warm serving plates. Reheat any remaining glaze and pour over fish. Garnish with chervil sprigs and serve with stir-fried vegetables, if desired.

Tuna with Tomato and Olive Salsa

SERVES 4

4 TABLESPOONS GREEN OLIVE PURÉE

115ML (4FL OZ) OLIVE OIL

3 GARLIC CLOVES, CRUSHED

*4 TUNA STEAKS, EACH WEIGHING
ABOUT 150G (5OZ)*

TOMATO AND OLIVE SALSA

15 BLACK OLIVES, STONED AND SLICED

4 TOMATOES, PEELED, SEEDED AND SLICED

*85G (3OZ) SUN-DRIED TOMATOES IN OIL,
DRAINED AND SLICED*

4 SPRING ONIONS, CHOPPED

14 BASIL LEAVES, TORN

PINCH SUGAR

◆ To make marinade, mix together green olive purée, olive oil and garlic in a shallow dish. Season with salt and pepper.

◆ Add tuna steaks to marinade and turn to coat evenly. Cover and refrigerate for 2 hours.

◆ To make tomato and olive salsa, combine black olives, tomatoes, sun-dried tomatoes, spring onions, basil leaves and a pinch of sugar. Refrigerate until required.

◆ Remove tuna steaks from marinade, reserving marinade for basting. Cook steaks on a prepared barbecue for about 5 minutes on each side, basting occasionally with marinade.

◆ Serve tuna at once with tomato and olive salsa.

Mesquite-smoked Monkfish

SERVES 4

115G (4FL OZ) EXTRA VIRGIN OLIVE OIL

4 TABLESPOONS WHITE WINE VINEGAR

4 GARLIC CLOVES, CRUSHED

2 TEASPOONS BLACK PEPPERCORNS, CRUSHED

2 TEASPOONS CHOPPED FENNEL FRONDS

PINCH SEA SALT

*4 PIECES MONKFISH TAIL WITH BONE, EACH
WEIGHING ABOUT 200G (7OZ)*

*ABOUT 1 CUP MESQUITE CHIPS,
SOAKED IN COLD WATER FOR 1 HOUR*

*COOKED NEW POTATOES, TO SERVE
(OPTIONAL)*

◆ To make marinade, mix olive oil, white wine vinegar, garlic, peppercorns, chopped fennel and sea salt together in a bowl.

◆ Place fish portions in a shallow dish and pour over marinade, turning fish to coat evenly. Cover and refrigerate for 2 hours.

◆ Drain soaked mesquite chips and scatter over the hot coals of a prepared barbecue.

◆ Remove fish from marinade, reserving marinade for basting. Cook fish on barbecue for about 15 minutes, or until cooked through, turning and basting occasionally.

◆ Serve at once, with new potatoes if desired.

Salmon with Ginger Dip

SERVES 4

4 SALMON FILLETS, EACH WEIGHING ABOUT 175G (6OZ), SKINNED

3 TABLESPOONS LIGHT SOY SAUCE

1 TABLESPOON DRY SHERRY

2.5CM (1IN) PIECE FRESH GINGER, PEELED AND CUT INTO THIN STRIPS

FRESHLY GROUND BLACK PEPPER

2 TABLESPOONS SWEET SHERRY

4 SPRING ONIONS, SHREDDED, TO GARNISH

LIGHTLY COOKED ASPARAGUS TIPS, TO SERVE (OPTIONAL)

◆ Using a sharp knife, lightly score top of salmon fillets in diagonal lines, taking care not to slice all the way through.

◆ Place salmon in a shallow dish. Mix together 2 tablespoons soy sauce, dry sherry and ginger strips and spoon over salmon. Cover and refrigerate for 1 hour.

◆ Remove salmon from marinade, season with pepper and place on the oiled barbecue rack. Cook for 2-3 minutes on each side.

◆ Meanwhile, make dip by mixing together sweet sherry and remaining 1 tablespoon soy sauce.

◆ Drain cooked salmon on absorbent kitchen paper and place on serving plates. Garnish with shredded spring onions and serve with dip, accompanied by asparagus tips if desired.

Cod with Vinegar Sauce

SERVES 4

1 TABLESPOON SUNFLOWER OIL

6 SHALLOTS, SLICED

2 TABLESPOONS WHITE RICE VINEGAR

2 TEASPOONS SUGAR

1 TABLESPOON LIGHT SOY SAUCE

300ML (10FL OZ) VEGETABLE STOCK

1 TEASPOON CORNFLOUR MIXED WITH 2 TEASPOONS WATER

4 COD STEAKS, EACH WEIGHING ABOUT 175G (6OZ)

SALT AND FRESHLY GROUND PEPPER

2 TABLESPOONS CHOPPED FRESH CHIVES

◆ Heat half the oil in a pan and stir-fry shallots for 2-3 minutes. Add vinegar, sugar and soy sauce and stir-fry for 1 minute.

◆ Pour in stock and bring to the boil. Simmer for 8-9 minutes or until thickened and slightly reduced. Stir in cornflour mixture and cook, stirring, until thickened. Keep warm.

◆ Season cod steaks on both sides and place on the rack of a prepared barbecue. Brush with remaining oil and cook for about 4 minutes on each side, or until cooked through. Drain on absorbent kitchen paper, then remove skin.

◆ Stir chives into vinegar sauce, spoon over cod steaks and serve.

Halibut Chargrilled in Banana Leaves

MAKES 4 SERVINGS

*1 POUND SKINLESS, BONELESS HALIBUT,
CUT INTO 1-INCH CUBES*

*4 PIECES BANANA LEAF, EACH ABOUT
12 INCHES SQUARE (SEE NOTE)*

OIL FOR BRUSHING

SPICY PASTE

1 LARGE DRIED CHILI

*2-INCH PIECE GALANGAL, PEELED AND
CHOPPED (SEE NOTE)*

2 LEMON GRASS STALKS, FINELY CHOPPED

2 GARLIC CLOVES, CRUSHED

1 SHALLOT, FINELY CHOPPED

2 KAFFIR LIME LEAVES, FINELY CHOPPED

1 TABLESPOON THAI FISH SAUCE

3 TABLESPOONS PEANUT OIL

Note: Galangal is used for its exotic taste, but you can substitute fresh ginger. Heavy-duty aluminum foil can be used instead of banana leaves; it will not need oiling.

◆ Prepare spicy paste. Soak red chili in hot water 10 minutes, then drain and chop finely.

◆ Place chili, galangal, lemon grass, garlic, shallot, lime leaves, fish sauce, and oil in a spice grinder or food processor and blend to a smooth paste.

◆ Transfer spicy paste to a shallow glass dish, add cubed fish, and toss to coat evenly. Cover and refrigerate 2 hours.

◆ Brush banana leaves with a little oil and divide marinated fish between them. Wrap up to form packages and secure with toothpicks.

◆ Brush outside of packages with a little oil and cook on a prepared grill about 10 minutes, until fish is cooked through.

Fish Gratins

½ TEASPOON DIJON-STYLE MUSTARD

1 TABLESPOON LEMON JUICE

1 TABLESPOON OLIVE OIL

DASH FRESHLY GRATED NUTMEG

SALT AND PEPPER

4 COD OR HADDOCK STEAKS, EACH
WEIGHING ABOUT 5 OUNCES

½ CUP FINELY SHREDDED SHARP
CHEDDAR CHEESE

3 TABLESPOONS FRESHLY GRATED
PARMESAN CHEESE

2 TABLESPOONS FINE FRESH BREADCRUMBS

PAPRIKA

◆ In a small bowl using a fork, beat together mustard and lemon juice, then gradually whisk in oil. Add nutmeg and season with salt and pepper.

◆ Cut squares of heavy-duty aluminum foil large enough to contain each fish fillet. Coat fillets in mustard mixture, then place on squares of foil.

◆ Cover fish with shredded Cheddar cheese. Mix together Parmesan cheese and breadcrumbs, sprinkle evenly onto fish, then season generously with pepper.

◆ Turn edges of foil over and pinch at the tops to seal. Place foil packages on the rack of a preheated grill 8 or 10 minutes until fish is cooked through and cheese has melted.

◆ Open packages and lightly sprinkle fish with paprika to serve.

Middle Eastern Monkfish

SERVES 4

2 GARLIC CLOVES, FINELY CHOPPED

6CM (2½IN) PIECE FRESH GINGER, FINELY CHOPPED

3 TABLESPOONS OLIVE OIL

2½ TABLESPOONS TOMATO PURÉE

1½ TEASPOONS GROUND CINNAMON

1 TEASPOON CARAWAY SEEDS, CRUSHED

SALT AND PEPPER

1KG (2¼LB) MONKFISH TAIL

½ SPANISH ONION, FINELY CHOPPED

COUSCOUS AND LEMON SLICES, TO SERVE (OPTIONAL)

◆ In a small bowl mix together garlic, ginger, olive oil, tomato purée, cinnamon, caraway seeds, salt and pepper.

◆ Remove fine skin from monkfish, then spread with spice mixture. Place fish in a shallow dish, cover and leave in a cool place for 1½ hours.

◆ Cut a piece of aluminium foil large enough to enclose fish. Make a bed of chopped onion on foil and place monkfish, and any spice paste left in dish, on top. Fold foil loosely over fish and seal edges tightly.

◆ Cook on the rack of a prepared barbecue for about 20-25 minutes. Open foil, baste fish with spice paste, reseal, turn package over and cook for a further 10-15 minutes as necessary.

◆ Serve monkfish on a bed of couscous and garnish with lemon slices, if desired.

Tuna with Ginger Vinaigrette

SERVES 4

2.5CM (1IN) PIECE FRESH GINGER, FINELY CHOPPED

2 LARGE SPRING ONIONS, WHITE AND SOME GREEN PARTS, FINELY SLICED

225ML (8FL OZ) OLIVE OIL

JUICE 2 LIMES

2 TABLESPOONS SOY SAUCE

2 TABLESPOONS SESAME OIL

1 BUNCH CORIANDER, A FEW SPRIGS RESERVED FOR GARNISH, REMAINDER FINELY CHOPPED

PEPPER

6 TUNA STEAKS, EACH WEIGHING ABOUT 150-175G (5-6OZ)

◆ To make ginger vinaigrette, in a bowl stir together ginger, spring onions, olive oil, lime juice and soy sauce, then whisk in sesame oil. Add chopped coriander and season with pepper. Set aside.

◆ Place tuna steaks on the rack of a prepared barbecue and cook for about 3-4 minutes on each side.

◆ Spoon some dressing onto 6 individual serving plates. Add tuna steaks and garnish with coriander sprigs. Serve any remaining dressing separately.

Salmon with Capers and Gazpacho Salsa

SERVES 4

3 TABLESPOONS OLIVE OIL

GRATED ZEST AND JUICE 1 LIME

1 TABLESPOON CAPERS IN BRINE, DRAINED

4 SALMON STEAKS

GAZPACHO SALSA

4 TOMATOES, PEELED, SEEDED AND DICED

½ LARGE CUCUMBER, DICED

½ ONION, DICED

½ RED PEPPER, DICED

1 TABLESPOON EACH CHOPPED FRESH
PARSLEY AND CORIANDER

1 TEASPOON CASTER SUGAR

2 TABLESPOONS RED WINE VINEGAR

◆ In a bowl mix together olive oil, lime zest and juice, capers and a pinch of salt. Place salmon steaks in a shallow dish and pour over marinade. Cover and refrigerate salmon for 2 hours, if time permits.

◆ To make salsa, put diced tomatoes, cucumber, onion and pepper in a bowl with chopped parsley and coriander, sugar and wine vinegar. Season to taste with salt and pepper. Cover and refrigerate until required.

◆ Remove salmon steaks from marinade and press a few capers into the flesh of each one. Reserve remaining marinade for basting.

◆ Cook salmon on a prepared barbecue for 4-5 minutes on each side, basting occasionally with marinade.

◆ Serve salmon hot with gazpacho salsa.

Pan-fried Fish with Lemon and Garlic Sauce

SERVES 6

6 SWORDFISH, HALIBUT OR SALMON STEAKS

225ML (8FL OZ) OLIVE OIL

12 BAY LEAVES, BRUISED

3 CARDAMOM PODS, BRUISED

1 TABLESPOON CHOPPED FRESH PARSLEY

1 TABLESPOON GROUND PAPRIKA

6 LEMON SLICES

JUICE 1 LEMON

1 GARLIC CLOVE, CRUSHED

1 TABLESPOON CHOPPED FRESH PARSLEY

SALT AND CAYENNE

◆ Wash and dry fish steaks and place in a large shallow dish.

◆ In a bowl mix together 150ml (5fl oz) olive oil, bay leaves, cardamom pods, chopped parsley, paprika and lemon slices. Pour over fish, cover and marinate for 2-3 hours, turning fish in marinade occasionally.

◆ To make sauce, beat lemon juice with remaining olive oil until thickened. Add garlic, parsley, salt and cayenne.

◆ Place a griddle over the barbecue, brush with oil and allow it to get really hot. Fry fish on both sides for 4-6 minutes, until golden and firm to the touch. Alternatively, place fish directly over the heat on the barbecue grid and cook for 4-6 minutes on each side.

◆ Serve fish steaks with plenty of lemon and garlic sauce poured over.

Aromatic Grilled Salmon

SERVES 6

6 MIDDLE-CUT SALMON CUTLETS,
EACH WEIGHING ABOUT 175G (6OZ)
AND 2CM (¾IN) THICK

SALT AND FRESHLY GROUND BLACK PEPPER

FLOUR FOR COATING

115G (4OZ) BUTTER

HANDFUL FRESH WINTER SAVORY OR
1-2 TABLESPOONS DRIED WINTER SAVORY,
MOISTENED

6 TEASPOONS LUMPFISH CAVIAR

WINTER SAVORY OR TARRAGON,
TO GARNISH

◆ Rinse salmon and pat dry on absorbent kitchen paper. Season to taste with salt and pepper. Dip in flour and shake off surplus.

◆ Melt butter and brush over salmon steaks. Place in a rectangular hinged basket. Sprinkle winter savory over the coals when they are hot.

◆ Barbecue fish on rack over hot coals for 4-5 minutes on each side, basting occasionally with melted butter. If cutlets start to brown too quickly, reduce heat or move basket to side of barbecue. Cutlets are cooked when it is easy to move centre bone.

◆ Serve salmon cutlets sprinkled with lumpfish caviar and garnished with winter savory or tarragon leaves.

Spiced Fish in Banana Leaves

SERVES 4

575G (1¼LB) WHITE FISH FILLETS

BANANA LEAVES

OIL FOR BRUSHING

SPICE PASTE

6 SHALLOTS, CHOPPED

2 GARLIC CLOVES, SMASHED

2 FRESH RED CHILLIES, CORED, SEEDED AND CHOPPED

2.5CM (1IN) PIECE FRESH GINGER, CHOPPED

4 CANDLENUTS OR CASHEW NUTS

½ TEASPOON TAMARIND PASTE

2 TEASPOONS GROUND CORIANDER

2 TEASPOONS GROUND CUMIN

¼ TEASPOON GROUND TURMERIC

PINCH SALT

◆ To make spice paste, put shallots, garlic, chillies, ginger, nuts, tamarind paste, coriander, cumin, turmeric and salt into a blender or food processor and mix to a paste.

◆ Cut fish into 10 x 5 x 1cm (4 x 2 x ½in) pieces. Coat the top of each piece thickly with spice paste.

◆ If using banana leaves, hold them with tongs over a flame to soften. Oil leaves thoroughly and cut into pieces to wrap around pieces of fish. Secure parcels with cocktail sticks. Alternatively, if banana leaves are not available, wrap fish in pieces of heavy-duty aluminium foil.

◆ Place fish parcels on barbecue and cook for 4-5 minutes on each side.

◆ Serve with lime wedges, and with banana leaf or foil partially torn away to reveal fish inside.

Blackened Sea Bass with Butter Sauce

4 SEA BASS FILLETS, EACH WEIGHING
150G (5OZ)

55G (2OZ) BUTTER, MELTED

LEMON WEDGES, TO SERVE

SKEWERED NEW POTATOES, TO SERVE
(SEE NOTE)

SPICE MIX

1 TEASPOON SALT

1 TEASPOON GARLIC GRANULES

1 TEASPOON DRIED PARSLEY

1 TEASPOON CHILLI POWDER

½ TEASPOON GROUND BAY LEAVES

1 TABLESPOON CAYENNE

GROUND BLACK PEPPER

BUTTER SAUCE

3 TABLESPOONS DRY WHITE WINE

2 TABLESPOONS WHITE WINE VINEGAR

55G (2OZ) BUTTER, DICED

150ML (5FL OZ) DOUBLE CREAM

1 TABLESPOON CHOPPED FRESH PARSLEY

1 TABLESPOON CHOPPED FRESH CHIVES

◆ To make spice mix, in a bowl combine salt, garlic granules, dried parsley, chilli powder, ground bay leaves, cayenne and black pepper. Transfer to a plate.

◆ Brush sea bass fillets all over with melted butter, then place on spice mix and turn to coat evenly. Cover and refrigerate fillets for 1 hour.

◆ Cook fish on the oiled rack of a prepared barbecue for 3-4 minutes on each side.

◆ Just before serving, make sauce. Place wine and vinegar in a saucepan and boil rapidly for 1-2 minutes to reduce by half.

◆ Whisk in butter, a piece at a time, over low heat. Add cream and whisk for 1-2 minutes, then stir in chopped parsley and chives.

◆ Serve sea bass with hot butter sauce and lemon wedges, accompanied by skewered new potatoes, if desired.

Note: To make skewered new potatoes, cook 16 baby new potatoes in boiling salted water for about 12 minutes. Toss in plenty of olive oil, salt and pepper while still warm, then thread onto 4 skewers and cook on the barbecue for 12-15 minutes, turning frequently.

Chargrilled Tuna Niçoise

SERVES 4

350G (12OZ) WAXY NEW POTATOES, SCRAPED

115G (4OZ) GREEN BEANS, HALVED

4 TUNA STEAKS, EACH WEIGHING 175G (6OZ)

1 LITTLE GEM LETTUCE

HANDFUL ROCKET LEAVES

225G (8OZ) CHERRY TOMATOES, HALVED

8 QUAILS' EGGS, HARD-BOILED AND HALVED

55G (2OZ) CAN ANCHOVIES IN OLIVE OIL, DRAINED

12 BLACK OLIVES

VINAIGRETTE

½ TEASPOON DIJON MUSTARD

1 TABLESPOON WHITE WINE VINEGAR

SALT AND FRESHLY GROUND BLACK PEPPER

115ML (4FL OZ) EXTRA VIRGIN OLIVE OIL

1 TABLESPOON CHOPPED FRESH CHIVES

◆ To make vinaigrette, whisk together mustard, vinegar, salt and pepper. Whisk in olive oil, then stir in chives. Set aside.

◆ Cook potatoes in boiling, salted water for 15 minutes, until tender. Drain, slice and return to pan. Add 1 tablespoon of vinaigrette to potatoes, mix gently and leave to cool.

◆ Cook beans in boiling salted water for 3-4 minutes until tender but still crisp. Drain, rinse under cold water and drain again. Add beans to potatoes and mix together.

◆ Brush tuna steaks on both sides with vinaigrette. Place on the rack of a prepared barbecue and cook for 4-5 minutes on each side until browned but still slightly pink in the centre.

◆ Meanwhile, arrange lettuce leaves and rocket on serving plates. Drizzle with a little vinaigrette. Arrange cooked potatoes and beans, tomatoes, hard-boiled eggs, anchovies and olives on top.

◆ Place a tuna steak on top of each plate of salad, pour over remaining vinaigrette and serve.

Oily Fish

Stuffed Sardines

SERVES 4-6

225G (8OZ) TRIMMED SPINACH LEAVES, WASHED

1 GARLIC CLOVE, CRUSHED

GRATED ZEST 1 LEMON

2 TABLESPOONS CHOPPED FRESH PARSLEY

25G (1OZ) PINE NUTS, TOASTED AND CHOPPED

2 TABLESPOONS RAISINS

8 ANCHOVY FILLETS CANNED IN OIL, DRAINED AND CHOPPED

115G (4OZ) FRESH BREADCRUMBS

55G (2OZ) FETA CHEESE, CRUMBLED

1/4 TEASPOON GROUND MIXED SPICE

2 TABLESPOONS OLIVE OIL

12 LARGE SARDINES, EACH WEIGHING ABOUT 115G (4OZ)

SALT AND PEPPER

LEMON WEDGES, TO GARNISH

◆ Place washed spinach leaves in a pan with no extra water and heat for 2-3 minutes until just wilted. Drain, squeeze out excess liquid and chop finely.

◆ In a bowl, mix together garlic, lemon zest, parsley, pine nuts, raisins, anchovies, breadcrumbs, feta, mixed spice and 1 tablespoon olive oil. Stir in wilted spinach and set aside for 1 hour to allow flavours to infuse.

◆ Wash and dry sardines and fill stomach cavities with spinach mixture. Brush with remaining oil and place on the prepared barbecue. Cook for about 4-5 minutes on each side until browned and firm to the touch.

◆ Serve hot with lemon wedges.

Tarama Sardines

SERVES 6

6 SARDINES, HEADS REMOVED

2 TABLESPOONS LEMON JUICE

FRESHLY GROUND BLACK PEPPER

3-4 TABLESPOONS TARAMASALATA

PARSLEY SPRIGS, TO GARNISH

◆ Rinse sardines and pat dry on absorbent kitchen paper. Brush insides with lemon juice and season to taste with black pepper. Carefully fill cavities with taramasalata.

◆ Place sardines in a hinged rectangular basket and barbecue over hot coals for 3-4 minutes on each side.

◆ Serve garnished with parsley sprigs.

Variation: Use small trout if sardines are not available and double the quantity of taramasalata.

Herrings in Oatmeal

SERVES 4

4 HERRINGS, EACH WEIGHING ABOUT 225G (8OZ), HEADS AND TAILS REMOVED

SALT AND PEPPER

1 LEMON, HALVED

115G (4OZ) MEDIUM OATMEAL

LEMON WEDGES, TO SERVE

MUSTARD SAUCE

85ML (3FL OZ) THICK MAYONNAISE

85ML (3FL OZ) PLAIN YOGURT

ABOUT 1 TABLESPOON DIJON MUSTARD

ABOUT 1½ TEASPOONS TARRAGON VINEGAR

◆ To make mustard sauce, in a small bowl, mix together mayonnaise and yogurt and stir in mustard and vinegar to taste. Spoon into a small serving bowl and chill lightly.

◆ Place one fish on a board, cut-side down and opened out. Press gently along backbone with your thumbs. Turn fish over and carefully lift away backbone and attached bones.

◆ Season fish with salt and pepper and squeeze lemon juice over both sides, then fold in half, skin-side outwards. Repeat with remaining fish.

◆ Coat fish evenly in oatmeal, pressing it in well but gently.

◆ Place herrings on prepared barbecue and cook for 3-4 minutes on each side until brown and crisp and flesh flakes easily. Serve hot with mustard sauce and lemon wedges.

Mediterranean Chargrilled Sardines

SERVES 4-6

12 SMALL SARDINES

12 SMALL STRIPS LEMON PEEL

12 SMALL ROSEMARY SPRIGS

4-6 LEMON WEDGES, TO SERVE

HERB AND LEMON OIL

4 TABLESPOONS EXTRA VIRGIN OLIVE OIL

2 TEASPOONS GRATED LEMON ZEST

JUICE 1 LEMON

1 TABLESPOON CHOPPED FRESH ROSEMARY

1 TABLESPOON CHOPPED FRESH THYME

SALT AND FRESHLY GROUND BLACK PEPPER

◆ Wash sardines and dry on absorbent kitchen paper. Stuff a small strip of lemon peel and a rosemary sprig into the cavity of each sardine.

◆ Thread three sardines onto each pair of skewers by pushing one skewer through a sardine just below the head and pushing the second skewer in just above the tail.

◆ To make herb and lemon oil, mix together in a bowl olive oil, lemon zest and juice, rosemary, thyme, salt and pepper.

◆ Brush herb and lemon oil liberally over sardines. Cook on a very hot barbecue for 3-4 minutes on each side, basting with more oil while they are cooking.

◆ Slide cooked sardines off skewers and serve two or three to each person, with lemon wedges.

Note: Use a metal fish rack that holds 6 or 12 sardines instead of skewers if preferred.

Sardines with Caponata

SERVES 4-6

12 LARGE SARDINES

JUICE 1 LEMON

OIL FOR BRUSHING

CAPONATA

6 TABLESPOONS OLIVE OIL

1 ONION, CHOPPED

1 GARLIC CLOVE, CHOPPED

2 CELERY STICKS, CHOPPED

1 TABLESPOON CHOPPED FRESH BASIL

1 MEDIUM AUBERGINE, DICED

55G (2OZ) PITTED GREEN OLIVES, HALVED

2 TABLESPOONS CAPERS

2 RIPE TOMATOES, CHOPPED

1½ TABLESPOONS RED WINE VINEGAR

1 TEASPOON SUGAR

2 TABLESPOONS PINE NUTS, TOASTED

◆ To make caponata, heat 2 tablespoons oil in a frying pan and fry onion, garlic, celery and basil for 5 minutes until browned. Transfer mixture to a bowl with a slotted spoon.

◆ Add remaining oil to pan and fry aubergine for 5-6 minutes until golden. Add to onion and celery mixture with olives and capers.

◆ Place tomatoes, vinegar and sugar in a saucepan and bring to the boil. Cover and simmer gently for 15 minutes. Stir in vegetable mixture and pine nuts and season to taste. Set aside to cool slightly.

◆ Gradually work in oil to form a thick sauce. (Thin with 2-3 tablespoons boiling water if too thick.) Transfer to a bowl, cover and set aside.

◆ Brush inside and outside of sardines with oil. Season and squeeze over a little lemon juice. Cook sardines on a prepared barbecue for 4-5 minutes on each side until charred and cooked through.

◆ Spoon caponata mixture onto individual serving plates, top each with 2-3 sardines and serve at once.

Mackerel and Gooseberries

SERVES 4

450G (1LB) GOOSEBERRIES

1 TEASPOON FENNEL SEEDS

2 MACKEREL, EACH WEIGHING 450G (1LB) AND CUT INTO 2 FILLETS

1 TABLESPOON OLIVE OIL

SALT AND FRESHLY GROUND BLACK PEPPER

1 TABLESPOON PASTIS OR OTHER ANISEED-FLAVOURED LIQUEUR

1 TEASPOON SUGAR

25G (1OZ) BUTTER, DICED

PARSLEY SPRIGS, TO GARNISH

◆ Put gooseberries and fennel seeds in a saucepan with just enough water to cover. Bring to the boil, then simmer for 7-10 minutes, until very soft.

◆ With the point of a sharp knife, make three slashes in each mackerel fillet. Season fish, brush with oil on each side and cook on a prepared barbecue for 10 minutes, turning once.

◆ Reserve a few gooseberries for garnish. Press remainder through a nylon sieve into a saucepan, pressing hard to extract all the juice.

◆ Add pastis, sugar and salt and pepper and heat gently, gradually beating in butter.

◆ Pour gooseberry sauce over fish, garnish with reserved gooseberries and parsley and serve.

Mackerel with Mustard

SERVES 4

2 TABLESPOONS DIJON MUSTARD

4 TABLESPOONS FINELY CHOPPED FRESH CORIANDER

2 GARLIC CLOVES, FINELY CRUSHED

2-3 TEASPOONS LEMON JUICE

SALT AND PEPPER

4 MACKEREL, EACH WEIGHING ABOUT 300G (10OZ)

ROLLED OATS FOR COATING

LEMON WEDGES AND CORIANDER SPRIGS, TO GARNISH

TOMATO, FENNEL AND THYME SALAD, TO SERVE (OPTIONAL)

◆ In a bowl, mix together mustard, coriander, garlic and lemon juice and season with salt and pepper.

◆ Using the point of a sharp knife, cut 3 slashes in both sides of each mackerel. Spoon mustard mixture into slashes and sprinkle with a few rolled oats.

◆ Wrap each fish in a large piece of aluminium foil and fold edges of foil together to seal tightly.

◆ Place foil packages on the barbecue rack over hot coals for 5 minutes. Open foil, turn fish, reseal packages and cook for a further 2-3 minutes. Open foil, place fish directly on rack and cook for a further 2-3 minutes until cooked.

◆ Garnish with lemon wedges and coriander sprigs and serve with tomato, fennel and thyme salad, if desired.

Sardines with Avgolemono Sauce

SERVES 4

1 KG (2¼LB) SARDINES

2 TABLESPOONS COARSE SEA SALT

1 TABLESPOON CHOPPED FRESH OREGANO

1 TABLESPOON CHOPPED FRESH PARSLEY

1 TABLESPOON CHOPPED FRESH FENNEL

LEMON SLICES, TO GARNISH

AVGOLEMONO SAUCE

400ML (14FL OZ) FISH STOCK

SALT AND PEPPER

3 TEASPOONS CORNFLOUR

2 LARGE EGG YOLKS

JUICE 1 LEMON

◆ Slash each sardine twice on each side and sprinkle with sea salt. Put chopped fresh oregano, parsley and fennel inside cavities. Set aside for 30 minutes.

◆ To make avgolemono sauce, put fish stock in a saucepan, season with salt and pepper and heat. In a bowl, mix cornflour with a little water. Whisk hot stock into cornflour mixture and return to pan. Cook gently for 10-15 minutes, stirring, until sauce thickens.

◆ In a bowl, beat egg yolks. Stir in lemon juice. Add a little hot sauce, then return sauce to pan. Cook gently, without boiling, until thickened.

◆ Place sardines onto rack of prepared barbecue and cook for 1½-2 minutes on each side until skins are brown and crisp.

◆ Garnish fish with lemon slices and serve with sauce.

Mackerel with Cucumber Raita

SERVES 4

1 GARLIC CLOVE, FINELY CRUSHED

½ TEASPOON HARISSA OR PINCH CHILLI POWDER

2 TEASPOONS GROUND CUMIN

2 TABLESPOONS LIGHT OLIVE OIL

SQUEEZE LEMON JUICE

SALT AND PEPPER

4 MACKEREL

CUCUMBER RAITA

½ CUCUMBER, PEELED

SALT

175ML (6FL OZ) GREEK-STYLE YOGURT

1¼ TABLESPOONS CHOPPED FRESH MINT

◆ To make raita, halve cucumber lengthways, scoop out seeds and thinly slice flesh. Spread flesh in a colander, sprinkle with salt and leave to drain for 30 minutes.

◆ Rinse cucumber, dry with absorbent kitchen paper and mix with yogurt and mint. Cover and chill for 2 hours.

◆ Put garlic in a mortar or small bowl, then pound in harissa or chilli powder, cumin and oil, using a pestle or the end of a rolling pin. Add lemon juice and season with salt and pepper.

◆ With the point of a sharp knife, cut 2 slashes in each side of mackerel. Spread spiced oil mixture over fish and leave for 15-30 minutes.

◆ Cook fish on prepared barbecue for 7-8 minutes on each side. Serve with cucumber raita.

Malaysian Mackerel with Spicy Peanut Sauce

SERVES 6

*4 tablespoons sambal oelek
(hot pepper condiment)*

4 tablespoons groundnut oil

2 teaspoons soft brown sugar

2 garlic cloves, crushed

Juice 2 limes

*6 medium mackerel, each weighing
about 200g (7oz)*

SPICY PEANUT SAUCE

*1 tablespoon tamarind concentrate,
mixed with 115ml (4fl oz) water*

4 teaspoons soft brown sugar

2 spring onions, chopped

1 lemon grass stalk, chopped

1 garlic clove, crushed

1 tablespoon sambal oelek

*85g (3oz) salted peanuts,
coarsely ground*

150ml (5fl oz) coconut milk

◆ In a small bowl mix together sambal oelek, groundnut oil, soft brown sugar, garlic and lime juice.

◆ Make several deep slashes in flesh of each mackerel and place fish in a large shallow dish. Pour over marinade and turn fish to coat well. Cover and refrigerate for at least 2 hours.

◆ To make peanut sauce, place tamarind concentrate, soft brown sugar, spring onions, lemon grass, garlic and sambal oelek in a saucepan. Bring to the boil, then reduce heat and simmer for 5 minutes.

◆ Add peanuts and cook for a further minute, then stir in coconut milk and simmer for a further 2 minutes. Set aside.

◆ Remove mackerel from marinade, reserving marinade for basting. Cook fish in a wire frame on a prepared barbecue for about 15 minutes, turning and basting fish as they cook.

◆ Serve fish with warm spicy peanut sauce.

Sardines with Coriander

SERVES 4

1kg (2¼lb) sardines (at least 12)

4 tablespoons olive oil

Grated zest 1½ limes

1½ tablespoons lime juice

¾ teaspoon finely crushed, toasted coriander seeds

3 tablespoons chopped fresh coriander

Salt and pepper

Coriander sprigs, to garnish

Lime wedges, to serve

◆ Put sardines in a shallow, nonmetallic dish. Thoroughly whisk together oil, lime zest and juice, crushed coriander seeds, chopped coriander and salt and pepper.

◆ Pour coriander mixture over sardines and leave for 1 hour, turning sardines over once.

◆ Remove sardines from dish and cook on a prepared barbecue for 4-5 minutes on each side, basting with coriander mixture.

◆ Serve sardines garnished with coriander sprigs and accompanied by lime wedges.

Kebabs

Tandoori Seafood Kebabs

SERVES 4

2 PLAICE, SKINNED AND FILLETED

16 LARGE RAW PRAWNS,
PEELED AND DEVEINED

450G (1LB) COD FILLET,
SKINNED AND DICED

2 LIMES, CUT INTO WEDGES

GREEN SALAD AND NAAN BREAD,
TO SERVE (OPTIONAL)

MARINADE

1 SMALL ONION, VERY FINELY CHOPPED

2 GARLIC CLOVES, CRUSHED

1 TEASPOON GRATED FRESH GINGER

1 TEASPOON MILD CURRY POWDER

1 TEASPOON PAPRIKA

1/4 TEASPOON CHILLI POWDER

1/4 TEASPOON TURMERIC

1 TABLESPOON LEMON JUICE

150ML (5FL OZ) GREEK-STYLE YOGURT

SALT AND PEPPER

◆ Wash and dry plaice fillets. Cut each one in half lengthways to make 16 thin strips of fish. Roll up and secure with cocktail sticks. Place in a shallow dish with prawns and diced cod.

◆ To make marinade, in a bowl mix together onion, garlic, ginger, curry powder, paprika, chilli powder, turmeric, lemon juice, yogurt and salt and pepper.

◆ Pour marinade over seafood. Cover and marinate for 30 minutes.

◆ Meanwhile, soak 8 bamboo skewers in cold water for 30 minutes. Drain and pat dry on absorbent kitchen paper.

◆ Thread fish, prawns and lime wedges alternately onto bamboo skewers. Place on a preheated barbecue and cook for about 8 minutes, turning and basting, until charred and cooked through.

◆ Place two kebabs on each plate. Serve with a green salad and naan bread and garnish with extra lime wedges, if desired.

Vietnamese Seafood Skewers

SERVES 6

12 SCALLOPS

12 LARGE RAW PEELED PRAWNS

*225G (8OZ) FIRM WHITE FISH FILLET,
SUCH AS HALIBUT, COD OR MONKFISH,
CUT INTO 12 CUBES*

1 MEDIUM ONION, CUT INTO 12 PIECES

*1 RED OR GREEN PEPPER, CUT INTO
12 CUBES*

*115ML (4FL OZ) DRY WHITE WINE
OR SHERRY*

1 TABLESPOON CHOPPED DILL

1 TABLESPOON CHOPPED HOLY BASIL LEAVES

1 TABLESPOON LIME JUICE OR VINEGAR

SALT AND FRESHLY GROUND BLACK PEPPER

VEGETABLE OIL FOR BRUSHING

SPICY FISH SAUCE

2 GARLIC CLOVES

*2 SMALL FRESH RED OR GREEN CHILLIES,
SEEDED AND CHOPPED*

1 TABLESPOON SUGAR

2 TABLESPOONS LIME JUICE

2 TABLESPOONS FISH SAUCE

◆ To make spicy fish sauce, pound garlic and chillies until finely ground using a pestle and mortar. Place in a bowl and add sugar, lime juice, fish sauce and 2-3 tablespoons water. Blend well and set aside.

◆ In a bowl, mix scallops, prawns, fish, onion and red or green pepper. In a small bowl or jug, mix together wine or sherry, dill, basil, lime juice or vinegar, salt and pepper. Pour over seafood and vegetables and leave to marinate in a cool place for at least 2-3 hours (the longer the better).

◆ Meanwhile, soak 6 bamboo skewers in hot water for 25-30 minutes.

◆ Thread seafood and vegetables alternately onto skewers so that each skewer has 2 pieces of each ingredient. Brush each filled skewer with a little oil.

◆ Cook on a prepared barbecue for 5-6 minutes, turning frequently. Serve hot with fish sauce as a dip.

Mexican Fish Kebabs with Guacamole

SERVES 4

4 TABLESPOONS CHOPPED CORIANDER

4 TABLESPOONS OLIVE OIL

JUICE 3 LIMES

4 TEASPOONS PAPRIKA

1 FRESH RED CHILLI, SEEDED AND
FINELY CHOPPED

575G (1¼LB) RED SNAPPER FILLETS

4 MINI RED PEPPERS, HALVED

2 ONIONS, EACH CUT INTO 8 WEDGES

GUACAMOLE

2 AVOCADOS

JUICE 1 LARGE LIME

½ ONION, FINELY CHOPPED

6 TABLESPOONS TORN CORIANDER LEAVES

◆ To make marinade, place chopped coriander, olive oil, lime juice, paprika and chopped red chilli in a shallow glass bowl and mix well.

◆ Cut fish fillets into chunks, add to marinade and turn to coat evenly. Cover and refrigerate for 2 hours.

◆ To make guacamole, mash avocados with lime juice. Stir in chopped onion and coriander leaves and season with salt and pepper. Refrigerate until required.

◆ Remove fish from marinade, reserving marinade for basting. Thread fish onto skewers, alternating with peppers and onions wedges.

◆ Cook kebabs on a prepared barbecue for about 10 minutes, turning and brushing them with reserved marinade. Serve at once with guacamole.

Scallops with Tindooris

SERVES 6-8

1kg (2¼LB) FRESH OR FROZEN SCALLOPS,
THAWED IF FROZEN

12 TINDOORIS

150ML (5FL OZ) OLIVE OIL

1 TABLESPOON LEMON JUICE

1 TABLESPOON LIME JUICE

¼ TEASPOON LEMON PEPPER

¼ TEASPOON ONION SALT

LEMON AND LIME SLICES, TO GARNISH

◆ Remove and discard any dark veins from scallops. Rinse scallops and pat dry with absorbent kitchen paper.

◆ Rinse tindooris and halve lengthways. Add to a saucepan of fast-boiling water and cook for 1 minute. Drain and leave to cool.

◆ In a large bowl combine olive oil, lemon and lime juice, lemon pepper and onion salt. Add scallops and leave for 1 hour, stirring occasionally. Add tindooris and leave for a further 15 minutes.

◆ Thread scallops and tindooris onto oiled skewers and barbecue on a rack over medium coals for 5-10 minutes, basting frequently with marinade. Scallops are cooked when opaque.

Monkfish Kebabs with Cherry Tomato Salsa

SERVES 4

1 SMALL RED ONION, FINELY CHOPPED

1 GARLIC CLOVE, CRUSHED

2 TABLESPOONS CHOPPED FRESH CORIANDER

4 TABLESPOONS CHOPPED FRESH PARSLEY

1 TEASPOON GROUND CUMIN

1 TEASPOON PAPRIKA

1/4 TEASPOON CHILLI POWDER

PINCH SAFFRON THREADS

4 TABLESPOONS OLIVE OIL

JUICE 1 LEMON

1/2 TEASPOON SALT

700G (1 1/2LB) MONKFISH FILLETS, SKINNED

FLAT-LEAF PARSLEY SPRIGS AND CHIVES, TO GARNISH

CHERRY TOMATO SALSA

225G (8OZ) RED AND YELLOW CHERRY TOMATOES

1 SMALL RED ONION, THINLY SLICED

1 QUANTITY VINAIGRETTE (SEE PAGE 44)

1 SMALL FRESH GREEN CHILLI, SEEDED AND SLICED

1 TABLESPOON CHOPPED FRESH CHIVES

◆ In a large bowl mix together onion, garlic, coriander, parsley, cumin, paprika, chilli powder, saffron, olive oil, lemon juice and salt.

◆ Cut monkfish into cubes and add to marinade. Mix well, cover and leave in a cool place to marinate for 1 hour.

◆ Meanwhile, make cherry tomato salsa. Halve tomatoes and put in a bowl. Add onion, vinaigrette, chilli and chives. Mix well and leave to stand for 30 minutes.

◆ Thread monkfish onto 4 skewers and place on a low rack of a prepared barbecue. Spoon over a little marinade. Cook for 3 minutes on each side until cooked through and lightly browned.

◆ Garnish with parsley sprigs and chives and serve with tomato salsa.

Lime Fish Skewers

SERVES 4

350G (12OZ) MONKFISH TAILS, SKINNED AND CUT INTO 2CM (³⁄₄IN) CUBES

350G (12OZ) TROUT FILLETS, SKINNED AND CUT INTO 2CM (³⁄₄IN) CUBES

2 LIMES

1 TEASPOON SESAME OIL

LARGE PINCH FIVE-SPICE POWDER

FRESHLY GROUND BLACK PEPPER

STRIPS LIME PEEL, TO GARNISH

◆ Place monkfish and trout in a shallow dish. Juice one lime and grate zest. Mix juice and zest with sesame oil and five-spice powder. Pour over fish, cover and chill for 30 minutes.

◆ Soak 4 bamboo skewers in cold water. Halve and quarter remaining lime lengthways and halve each quarter to make 8 wedges. Slice each piece of lime in half crossways to make 16 small pieces.

◆ Thread monkfish, trout and lime pieces onto skewers and place on the rack of a prepared barbecue. Brush with marinade and season with pepper. Cook for 2 minutes on each side, brushing occasionally with marinade to prevent drying out.

◆ Drain on absorbent kitchen paper, then place each kebab on a separate serving plate and garnish with lime peel to serve.

Swordfish Kebabs with Chermoula

◆ To make chermoula, crush garlic with salt using a pestle and mortar. Place in a blender or food processor.

◆ Add lemon juice, cumin, paprika, red chilli, coriander and parsley to blender or food processor. Process briefly, then, with the motor running, gradually add olive oil and reduce to a coarse purée. Transfer to a bowl.

◆ Cut swordfish into 2.5cm (1in) cubes and add to chermoula mixture. Mix well to coat. Cover and leave in a cool place to marinate for 1 hour.

◆ Thread fish cubes onto skewers and place on the rack of a preheated barbecue. Spoon marinade over fish.

◆ Cook over hot coals for 3-4 minutes on each side, until fish is lightly browned and flakes easily when tested with the sharp point of a knife.

Variation: Instead of swordfish steaks, try using monkfish or raw tiger prawns for this recipe.

Prawn and Monkfish Kebabs with Coconut Salsa

SERVES 6

18 LARGE RAW PRAWNS

450G (1LB) MONKFISH FILLETS

4 LIMES, SLICED

SALSA

200ML (7FL OZ) OLIVE OIL

2 TEASPOONS SESAME OIL, PLUS EXTRA FOR BASTING

8 SPRING ONIONS, TRIMMED AND FINELY CHOPPED

2 TABLESPOONS CHOPPED FRESH CORIANDER

ZEST AND JUICE 2 LIMES

1-2 DRIED RED CHILLIES, CRUSHED

55G (2OZ) DESICCATED COCONUT

◆ To make salsa, heat olive and sesame oils together in a small pan and sauté spring onion and coriander for 2 minutes.

◆ Remove from heat and stir in lime zest and juice, dried red chillies, and desiccated coconut. Transfer to a small dish and leave to cool.

◆ Wash and dry prawns and, if desired, remove heads and shells. Cut monkfish into 2.5cm (1in) pieces.

◆ Thread prawns, monkfish and lime slices alternately onto metal skewers and brush all over with sesame oil.

◆ Place skewers on a prepared barbecue and cook for 6-8 minutes, turning and basting occasionally, until prawns and monkfish are lightly charred and cooked through.

◆ Serve at once with coconut salsa.

Scallop Brochettes with Ginger and Orange Butter

SERVES 4

JUICE 2 ORANGES

7 TEASPOONS GRATED FRESH GINGER

4 TABLESPOONS VEGETABLE OIL

4 SPRING ONIONS, FINELY CHOPPED

2 GARLIC CLOVES, CRUSHED

SALT AND GROUND BLACK PEPPER

16 LARGE SCALLOPS

115G (4OZ) BUTTER, SOFTENED

1 TABLESPOON GRATED ORANGE ZEST

SALT AND FRESHLY GROUND BLACK PEPPER

4 LONG STRIPS ORANGE PEEL

350G (12OZ) COURGETTES, CANNELLED AND CUT INTO 12 CHUNKS

◆ To make marinade, in a large shallow bowl mix together orange juice, reserving 1 tablespoon for butter, 4 teaspoons grated fresh ginger, oil, spring onions, garlic and salt and pepper. Add scallops to marinade and turn to coat evenly. Cover and refrigerate for 2 hours.

◆ To make ginger and orange butter, mix together softened butter, remaining ginger and orange juice, orange zest and salt and pepper. Place butter in a sausage shape on a piece of greaseproof paper or cling film. Roll up to form a cylinder and refrigerate until butter hardens.

◆ Remove scallops from marinade, reserving marinade for basting. Alternately thread 4 scallops, a strip of orange peel and 3 chunks of courgette onto each skewer.

◆ Cook brochettes on a prepared, medium-hot barbecue for 8-10 minutes, turning and brushing them frequently with marinade. Serve hot brochettes with discs of flavoured butter.

Turmeric Prawn and Pineapple Skewers

SERVES 4

1 LEMON GRASS STALK, FINELY CHOPPED

2.5CM (1IN) PIECE FRESH GINGER, PEELED AND GRATED

2 GARLIC CLOVES, CRUSHED

2 TABLESPOONS GROUNDNUT OIL

1 TABLESPOON LEMON JUICE

1 TEASPOON TURMERIC

PINCH EACH SUGAR, SALT AND PEPPER

24 RAW TIGER PRAWNS, PEELED BUT WITH TAILS LEFT ON

225G (8OZ) FRESH PINEAPPLE

16 BULBOUS WHITE PARTS OF SPRING ONIONS

◆ Place lemon grass, ginger, garlic, oil, lemon juice, turmeric, sugar, salt and pepper in a food processor and blend to a paste.

◆ Transfer paste to a large bowl, add prawns and turn to coat evenly. Refrigerate for 2-3 hours or overnight.

◆ Remove prawns from marinade, reserving marinade for basting. Cut pineapple into 16 chunks and thread onto skewers, alternating with prawns and spring onions.

◆ Cook skewers on a prepared barbecue for 8-10 minutes, turning and basting them while they cook. Serve at once.

Swordfish and Cherry Tomato Kebabs

SERVES 4

JUICE ½ LEMON

4 TABLESPOONS OLIVE OIL

1 TABLESPOON CHOPPED FRESH FENNEL

1 TABLESPOON CHOPPED FRESH CHIVES

1 GARLIC CLOVE, CRUSHED

SALT AND PEPPER

450G (1LB) SWORDFISH

1 SMALL ONION

16 CHERRY TOMATOES

LEMON SLICES AND FRESH HERBS,
TO GARNISH

◆ In a bowl mix together lemon juice, oil, fennel, chives, garlic, salt and pepper. Cut swordfish into 2cm (¾in) cubes. Place in bowl of marinade and leave for 1 hour.

◆ Cut onion into quarters and separate layers.

◆ Remove fish from marinade, reserving marinade for basting. Thread swordfish, onion and cherry tomatoes alternately onto 8 skewers.

◆ Place skewers on the rack of a prepared barbecue and cook for 5-10 minutes, turning occasionally and basting with reserved marinade.

◆ Serve kebabs garnished with lemon slices and herb sprigs.

Turkish Swordfish Kebabs

SERVES 4

4 TABLESPOONS LEMON JUICE

4 TABLESPOONS OLIVE OIL

1 SHALLOT, FINELY CHOPPED

3 FRESH BAY LEAVES, TORN

$1\frac{1}{2}$ TEASPOONS PAPRIKA

SALT AND PEPPER

575G ($1\frac{1}{4}$LB) SWORDFISH, CUT INTO
2.5 X 4CM (1 X $1\frac{1}{2}$IN) CUBES

PARSLEY SPRIGS, TO GARNISH

LEMON SAUCE

3 TABLESPOONS OLIVE OIL

3 TABLESPOONS LEMON JUICE

3 TABLESPOONS CHOPPED FRESH PARSLEY

SALT AND PEPPER

◆ To prepare marinade, mix together lemon juice, olive oil, shallot, bay leaves, paprika, salt and pepper.

◆ Lay swordfish in a single layer in a wide, shallow, nonmetallic dish. Pour over marinade, turn fish so it is evenly coated, then cover and leave in a cool place for 4-5 hours, turning fish occasionally.

◆ To make lemon sauce, mix together olive oil, lemon juice and chopped parsley and season with salt and pepper. Set aside.

◆ Remove fish from marinade and thread onto 4 skewers. Barbecue for 4-5 minutes on each side, basting frequently.

◆ Serve kebabs with sauce, garnished with parsley sprigs.

Swordfish Kebabs with Puy Lentils

SERVES 4

115G (4OZ) PUY LENTILS, SOAKED

100ML (3½FL OZ) OLIVE OIL

1 RED ONION, DICED

1 SMALL RED PEPPER, SEEDED AND DICED

1 GARLIC CLOVE, CRUSHED

JUICE 1 LEMON

2 TABLESPOONS CHOPPED FRESH BASIL

55G (2OZ) PITTED BLACK OLIVES, CHOPPED

700G (1½LB) SWORDFISH STEAK, DICED

◆ Drain lentils well, place in a pan and cover with cold water. Bring to the boil, then simmer gently for 35-40 minutes until tender. Drain.

◆ Heat 2 tablespoons olive oil in a frying pan and fry onion, pepper and garlic for 5 minutes. Add lemon juice, lentils, basil and olives and simmer gently for 3 minutes. Keep warm.

◆ Thread cubed swordfish onto 8 small skewers. Brush with a little remaining oil and place on the rack of a prepared barbecue. Cook for 4-5 minutes, turning and basting, until golden and firm to the touch.

◆ Stir remaining oil into lentil mixture and heat through. Spoon onto warmed plates and top with kebabs. Serve at once.

Tuna Fish Saté

SERVES 6

900G (2LB) FRESH TUNA STEAKS

3 TABLESPOONS LIGHT SOY SAUCE

1 TABLESPOON SESAME OIL

1 TABLESPOON CLEAR HONEY

1 TABLESPOON DRY SHERRY

JUICE 1 LIME

1 GARLIC CLOVE, CRUSHED

2.5CM (1IN) PIECE FRESH GINGER, GRATED

SATÉ SAUCE

4 TABLESPOONS RAW PEANUTS, GROUND

JUICE 1 LIME

15G (½OZ) CREAMED COCONUT

¼ TEASPOON CAYENNE

PINCH SUGAR

◆ Wash and dry tuna and cut into 1cm (½ in) cubes. Place in a large shallow dish.

◆ To make marinade, blend together soy sauce, sesame oil, honey, sherry, lime juice, garlic, grated ginger and 2 tablespoons water. Pour over fish. Cover and leave for 1-2 hours, turning fish occasionally.

◆ Drain and reserve marinade and thread 6 cubes of tuna onto each skewer. Cover and keep cool.

◆ To make sauce, put 6 tablespoons reserved marinade into a small pan and bring to the boil. Stir in ground peanuts, lime juice, creamed coconut, cayenne, a pinch of sugar and 2 tablespoons water.

◆ Simmer sauce over a low heat until coconut melts and sauce thickens slightly. Transfer to a small bowl and leave to cool.

◆ Cook tuna saté over a hot barbecue for 5-6 minutes, turning frequently and basting with remaining marinade until cooked. Serve with sauce.

Seafood Brochettes with Saffron Sauce

SERVES 4

350G (12OZ) SKINLESS, BONELESS
SALMON STEAK

350G (12OZ) SKINLESS, BONELESS
MONKFISH

16 LARGE RAW PRAWNS

4 TABLESPOONS SUNFLOWER OIL

8 TABLESPOONS CHOPPED FRESH CHERVIL

SAFFRON SAUCE

1 TABLESPOON SUNFLOWER OIL

2 SHALLOTS, FINELY CHOPPED

550ML (20 FL OZ) DRY WHITE WINE

1/2 TEASPOON SAFFRON THREADS, SOAKED
IN 2 TABLESPOONS BOILING WATER

300ML (10FL OZ) SINGLE CREAM

2 TABLESPOONS CHOPPED FRESH CHERVIL

2 TABLESPOONS CHOPPED FRESH CHIVES

◆ Cut salmon and monkfish into 16 chunks each. Place fish and prawns in a shallow glass dish.

◆ To make marinade, mix sunflower oil with chopped chervil and season with salt and pepper. Pour over seafood and toss to coat evenly. Cover and refrigerate for 2 hours.

◆ To make saffron sauce, heat oil in a saucepan and sauté shallots for 3 minutes. Add wine and saffron with water, bring to the boil and boil steadily for 10-12 minutes, until liquid has reduced to about one quarter of its original amount.

◆ Add cream and reduce again for 4-5 minutes. Add chervil, chives and seasoning and heat for a further 30 seconds. Set aside.

◆ Remove fish and prawns from marinade, reserving marinade for basting, and divide them equally between 8 skewers. Cook on the oiled rack of a prepared barbecue for 8-10 minutes, turning and brushing with marinade.

◆ Reheat sauce and serve it at once with brochettes.

Seared Scallop and Rosemary Kebabs

SERVES 8 AS A STARTER

4 TABLESPOONS WALNUT OIL

2 TABLESPOONS SHERRY VINEGAR

1 SMALL BUNCH BASIL

55G (2OZ) SUN-DRIED TOMATOES IN OIL,
DRAINED AND FINELY CHOPPED

FRESHLY GROUND BLACK PEPPER

48 BAY OR SMALL SCALLOPS

16 ROSEMARY SPRIGS

ROCKET LEAVES, TO SERVE

◆ To make marinade, whisk together walnut oil and sherry vinegar. Chop basil leaves and discard stems. Stir basil into oil and vinegar with sun-dried tomatoes. Season with black pepper. Set aside.

◆ Thread 3 scallops onto each rosemary sprig. Place in a shallow dish, pour dressing over and turn scallops to coat in dressing. Leave in a cool place for 30 minutes.

◆ Remove scallops from marinade and cook on the barbecue over hot coals for about 2 minutes, turning and basting with remaining marinade.

◆ Serve on a bed of rocket leaves.

Malaysian Prawn Balls

SERVES 8 AS A STARTER

700G (1½LB) LARGE RAW UNPEELED PRAWNS

1 GARLIC CLOVE, CHOPPED

1½ TABLESPOONS FISH SAUCE

½ TEASPOON LIGHT BROWN SUGAR

2 TEASPOONS GROUNDNUT OIL

1 TABLESPOON CORNFLOUR

1 EGG, BEATEN

SALT AND FRESHLY GROUND BLACK PEPPER

40G (1½OZ) DESICCATED COCONUT

2 TABLESPOONS DRIED BREADCRUMBS

CORIANDER SPRIGS, TO GARNISH

DIPPING SAUCE

1 GARLIC CLOVE, MASHED WITH SMALL PINCH SALT

4 TABLESPOONS LIGHT SOY SAUCE

2½ TABLESPOONS LIME JUICE

1 TABLESPOON VERY FINELY SLICED SPRING ONION

1 TEASPOON LIGHT BROWN SUGAR

1-2 DROPS CHILLI SAUCE

◆ Reserve 8 prawns in their shells and peel remainder. With the point of a sharp knife, cut a slit along the back of each peeled prawn. Remove and discard black intestinal thread.

◆ Put prawns in a food processor with garlic, fish sauce, sugar, oil, cornflour, egg, salt and pepper. Mix to a smooth purée. Transfer to a bowl, cover and chill for 1½ hours.

◆ Meanwhile, make dipping sauce. Mix garlic, soy sauce, lime juice, spring onion and sugar in a small bowl and add chilli sauce to taste.

◆ On a baking sheet, combine coconut and breadcrumbs. Wet the palms of your hands and roll prawn mixture into 2.5cm (1in) diameter balls. Coat balls in coconut mixture.

◆ Thread prawn balls onto oiled, long metal skewers, adding a reserved prawn to each skewer. Cook on a prepared barbecue, turning occasionally, for about 6 minutes, until balls are firm and whole prawns have turned pink.

◆ Garnish with coriander sprigs and serve with dipping sauce.

Squid and Prawn Kebabs with Garlic Mayonnaise

JUICE ½ LEMON

2 TEASPOONS CLEAR HONEY

2 TABLESPOONS OLIVE OIL

350G (12OZ) CLEANED SQUID, CUT INTO 0.5CM (¼IN) RINGS

8 LARGE RAW PEELED PRAWNS

SALT AND PEPPER

LEMON SLICES AND CHOPPED FRESH PARSLEY, TO GARNISH

GARLIC MAYONNAISE

4 GARLIC CLOVES

2 EGG YOLKS

300ML (10FL OZ) OLIVE OIL

JUICE ½ LEMON

◆ To make marinade, mix together lemon juice, honey and olive oil in a bowl. Add squid, cover and leave in a cool place for 6 hours.

◆ To make mayonnaise, crush garlic to a smooth pulp using a pestle and mortar. Put garlic in a blender or food processor with egg yolks and a little salt.

◆ With the motor running, gradually pour in half the oil. When mixture begins to thicken, add lemon juice and pepper. Add remaining oil.

◆ Drain squid and pat dry with absorbent kitchen paper. Thread onto wooden skewers, alternating with prawns. Season with salt and pepper.

◆ Cook kebabs on the barbecue for 4-5 minutes, turning occasionally, until golden.

◆ Cut lemon slices in half and dip cut edges in chopped parsley. Garnish kebabs with lemon slices and serve with garlic mayonnaise.

Skewered Tuna Rolls

SERVES 4

*700G (1½LB) FRESH TUNA, SLICED
0.5CM (¼IN) THICK*

1 TABLESPOON CHOPPED FRESH SAGE

1 TABLESPOON CHOPPED FRESH ROSEMARY

2 DRIED BAY LEAVES, CRUMBLED

1 TEASPOON DRIED CHILLI FLAKES

SALT AND FRESHLY GROUND BLACK PEPPER

FRESH BAY LEAVES

2 LEMONS, EACH CUT INTO 6 WEDGES

1 TABLESPOON OLIVE OIL

1 TABLESPOON LEMON JUICE

◆ Soak 4 bamboo skewers in cold water for 30 minutes.

◆ Meanwhile, place tuna slices between sheets of cling film and beat gently with a rolling pin until thin.

◆ Mix sage, rosemary, dried bay leaves and chilli flakes together. Sprinkle mixture over tuna slices and season with salt and pepper.

◆ Roll up each slice of tuna neatly. Thread onto bamboo skewers, alternately with fresh bay leaves and lemon wedges. Brush with olive oil and lemon juice, mixed together.

◆ Barbecue for 2-3 minutes on each side until just cooked.

Seafood

Spicy King Prawns with Guacamole

SERVES 6 AS A STARTER

2 GARLIC CLOVES, CRUSHED

*1 SMALL BUNCH CORIANDER,
FINELY CHOPPED*

JUICE 2 LIMES

*1 FRESH RED CHILLI, SEEDED AND
FINELY CHOPPED*

5 TABLESPOONS SUNFLOWER OIL

*24 LARGE RAW PRAWNS, PEELED
BUT WITH TAILS LEFT ON*

GUACAMOLE

1 GARLIC CLOVE, CRUSHED

4 TOMATOES, PEELED AND FINELY CHOPPED

*1 FRESH GREEN CHILLI, SEEDED AND
FINELY CHOPPED*

JUICE 1 LIME

*2 TABLESPOONS CHOPPED FRESH
CORIANDER*

SALT AND FRESHLY GROUND BLACK PEPPER

1 LARGE RIPE AVOCADO

◆ In a shallow nonmetallic dish, mix together garlic, coriander, lime juice, chilli and sunflower oil. Add prawns and mix well. Cover and chill for 1-2 hours, turning occasionally.

◆ To make guacamole, put garlic, tomatoes, chilli, lime juice, coriander and salt and pepper in a bowl and mix well.

◆ Halve avocado lengthways and remove stone. Using a teaspoon, scoop out flesh, taking care to scrape away dark green flesh closest to skin. Mash into tomato mixture.

◆ Remove prawns from marinade and arrange on barbecue rack. Cook for 2-3 minutes on each side, basting with marinade. Serve with guacamole.

Note: Don't prepare guacamole more than 30 minutes before serving or avocado will discolour.

Barbecued Prawns on Rice Vermicelli

SERVES 4

VEGETABLE OIL FOR DEEP-FRYING

115G (4OZ) RICE VERMICELLI

450G (1LB) RAW UNPEELED PRAWNS, HEADS REMOVED

2 TEASPOONS VEGETABLE OIL

2-3 SPRING ONIONS, CHOPPED

2-3 SMALL FRESH RED CHILLIES, CHOPPED

1 TABLESPOON ROASTED PEANUTS, CRUSHED, TO GARNISH

CORIANDER SPRIGS, TO GARNISH

SPICY FISH SAUCE (SEE PAGE 59), TO SERVE

◆ Heat oil for deep-frying to 150°C (300°F). Break vermicelli into short strands and deep-fry, a handful at a time, for 30-35 seconds, or until strands puff up and turn white. Remove vermicelli and drain, then place on a warm serving dish or plate.

◆ Cook prawns on the barbecue rack over hot coals for about 3-4 minutes. When cooked, arrange on bed of crispy rice vermicelli.

◆ Heat 2 teaspoons oil in a small saucepan until hot, removing from heat before it starts to smoke, and steep spring onions and chillies for a few minutes. Pour mixture all over prawns.

◆ Garnish with crushed peanuts and coriander sprigs and serve with spicy fish sauce as a dip.

Lobster with Fennel Sauce

SERVES 2

2 RAW LOBSTERS, EACH WEIGHING ABOUT
450G (1LB)

85ML (3FL OZ) OLIVE OIL

2 GARLIC CLOVES, CRUSHED

1 TABLESPOON CHOPPED FENNEL FRONDS

1 TEASPOON DRIED OREGANO

FENNEL SAUCE

150ML (5FL OZ) OLIVE OIL

JUICE 1 LEMON

1 GARLIC CLOVE, CRUSHED

2 TABLESPOONS CHOPPED FENNEL FRONDS

1 TABLESPOON CHOPPED FRESH PARSLEY

◆ Cut lobsters in half through the centre of their heads and bodies. Arrange cut-side up in a shallow dish.

◆ To make marinade, combine olive oil, garlic, fennel fronds and oregano in a bowl. Pour marinade over lobsters, cover and leave to marinate for 1 hour.

◆ To make fennel sauce, place oil in a bowl and gradually whisk in 4 tablespoons boiling water. Add lemon juice, garlic and chopped fennel and parsley. Continue to whisk for 1 minute until sauce is slightly thickened.

◆ Remove lobsters from marinade and place cut-side down on the barbecue rack. Cook for 8-10 minutes, until flesh has become opaque and shells have turned orange.

◆ Serve hot with fennel sauce.

Luxury Ginger Scampi

SERVES 4

150ML (5FL OZ) SALAD OIL

FINELY GRATED ZEST AND JUICE
1 SMALL LEMON

85ML (3FL OZ) SOY SAUCE

1 GARLIC CLOVE, CRUSHED

1 TEASPOON FINELY GRATED FRESH GINGER

1/2 TEASPOON DRIED MARJORAM

700G (1 1/2LB) RAW DUBLIN BAY
PRAWN TAILS (SEE NOTE)

MARJORAM SPRIGS AND LEMON SLICES,
TO GARNISH

◆ To make marinade, mix together salad oil, lemon juice and zest, soy sauce, garlic, ginger and dried marjoram in a large bowl.

◆ Wash prawns but leave shells intact if using unpeeled prawn tails. Add to bowl of marinade and turn to coat. Leave in a cool place for 2 hours, basting occasionally.

◆ Thread prawn tails crossways onto skewers and barbecue over hot coals for 7-10 minutes, turning frequently until prawns are opaque.

◆ Remove from skewers and serve at once, garnished with marjoram sprigs and lemon slices.

Note: Frozen, peeled raw prawn tails may be easier to obtain. These should be thawed before barbecuing.

Scallops with Rocket Pesto

SERVES 4

16 SHELLED SCALLOPS

OLIVE OIL FOR BRUSHING

SALT AND FRESHLY GROUND BLACK PEPPER

LEMON WEDGES AND ROCKET LEAVES, TO GARNISH

ROCKET PESTO

55G (2OZ) ROCKET

25G (1OZ) PINE NUTS

2 GARLIC CLOVES, CRUSHED

55G (2OZ) GRATED PARMESAN CHEESE

JUICE ½ LEMON

150ML (5FL OZ) OLIVE OIL

Note:: Double skewers are best for holding scallops in place on the barbecue.

◆ To make rocket pesto, put rocket, pine nuts, garlic, Parmesan cheese, and lemon juice in a food processor or blender and process until well blended.

◆ With the motor running, gradually pour in olive oil until combined. Season with salt and pepper. Transfer to a serving dish and set aside.

◆ Cut each scallop in half and thread scallops onto 8 pairs of skewers. Brush scallops with olive oil and season with salt.

◆ Place skewers on a prepared barbecue and cook for 1 minute on each side until browned on the outside but still moist in the centre.

◆ Garnish with lemon wedges and rocket leaves and serve with pesto.

Spanish-style Prawns

SERVES 4

450G (1LB) LARGE RAW PRAWNS, PEELED BUT WITH TAILS LEFT ON

5 TABLESPOONS EXTRA VIRGIN OLIVE OIL

½ GARLIC CLOVE, FINELY CRUSHED

JUICE 1 LEMON

SALT AND FRESHLY GROUND BLACK PEPPER

1 LARGE TOMATO, PEELED, SEEDED AND FINELY CHOPPED

½ SMALL RED CHILLI, SEEDED AND CHOPPED

1 TABLESPOON CHOPPED FRESH PARSLEY

PARSLEY SPRIGS AND LEMON SLICES AND ZEST, TO GARNISH

◆ Using a small sharp knife, make a fine cut along the spine of each prawn and remove black vein.

◆ Thread prawns onto small skewers and place in a shallow dish.

◆ In a small bowl, stir together 2 tablespoons oil, garlic, 1½ tablespoons lemon juice, salt and pepper. Pour over prawns and leave for 30 minutes.

◆ Lift prawns from dish and place on the rack of a prepared barbecue. Brush with any remaining marinade and cook for 3-4 minutes until pink.

◆ In another small bowl, stir together remaining oil and lemon juice, tomato, chilli, parsley and salt and pepper. Spoon over hot prawns.

◆ Serve prawns garnished with parsley sprigs and lemon slices and zest.

Crumbed Oysters with Piquant Tomato Dip

SERVES 4 AS A STARTER

55G (2OZ) BUTTER

70G (2½OZ) FRESH WHITE BREADCRUMBS

2 SPRING ONIONS, FINELY CHOPPED

1 TABLESPOON CHOPPED FRESH THYME

GENEROUS PINCH PAPRIKA

SALT AND FRESHLY GROUND BLACK PEPPER

16 FRESH OYSTERS

PIQUANT TOMATO DIP

450G (1LB) TOMATOES, ROUGHLY CHOPPED

4 SPRING ONIONS, FINELY CHOPPED

4 TEASPOONS HORSERADISH SAUCE

2 TEASPOONS WORCESTERSHIRE SAUCE

FEW DROPS TABASCO SAUCE

1 TEASPOON SUGAR

SALT AND FRESHLY GROUND BLACK PEPPER

◆ Prepare tomato dip. Place tomatoes in a food processor and blend briefly to produce a thick purée.

◆ Transfer tomatoes to a saucepan, add spring onions, horseradish, Worcestershire and Tabasco sauces, sugar, salt and pepper and bring to the boil.

◆ Boil sauce steadily for about 10 minutes until thick. Taste and adjust seasoning, if necessary, and set aside.

◆ Melt butter in a frying pan, add breadcrumbs and cook for 1 minute. Stir in spring onions, thyme, paprika and salt and pepper.

◆ Open oysters, leaving them on the half shell. Top each oyster with a little crispy breadcrumb mixture, making sure coating covers oysters.

◆ Cook oysters on a prepared barbecue for 4-5 minutes, until lightly cooked and heated through.

◆ Reheat tomato dip and serve with oysters.

Crab-stuffed Fishcakes

SERVES 6-8

700g (1½lb) minced white fish

1 small onion, very finely chopped

About 70g (2½oz) medium matzo meal

1 tablespoon ground almonds

Salt and pepper

3 eggs

115g (4oz) mixed white and brown crab meat

Sunflower oil for brushing

◆ In a small bowl, beat 2 eggs. In another bowl, combine fish, onion, 4 tablespoons matzo meal, ground almonds, salt and pepper. Bind mixture with beaten egg, adding more matzo meal if necessary to form a mixture that holds together when shaped.

◆ Divide mixture into 16 portions, shape into balls and flatten with the palm of the hand on a work surface sprinkled with matzo meal.

◆ Place a teaspoon of crab meat in the centres and wrap minced fish around to reform into balls. Press down lightly to make fishcake shapes.

◆ Beat remaining egg in a bowl and sprinkle remaining matzo meal onto a plate. Dip fishcakes in beaten egg, then in matzo meal.

◆ Brush both sides of each fishcake with sunflower oil and cook on a grill rack over hot coals for 6-8 minutes on each side.

Chargrilled Lobster with Herb Butter

SERVES 2

2 RAW LOBSTERS, EACH WEIGHING ABOUT 450G (1LB), SPLIT IN HALF LENGTHWAYS WITH CLAWS CRACKED

SALT AND GROUND BLACK PEPPER

HERB BUTTER

40G (1½OZ) BUTTER, SOFTENED

1 TABLESPOON CHOPPED FRESH CHERVIL

1 TEASPOON SNIPPED FRESH CHIVES

1 TEASPOON FINELY CHOPPED SHALLOT

SQUEEZE LEMON JUICE

SALT AND GROUND BLACK PEPPER

◆ To make herb butter, put butter, chervil, chives, shallot, lemon juice and salt and pepper into a bowl and beat together to combine.

◆ Place flavoured butter in a sausage shape on a piece of greaseproof paper or cling film. Roll up to produce a cylinder and refrigerate to harden.

◆ Season lobster flesh lightly with salt and pepper and cook lobster halves, cut-side down, on a prepared barbecue for 8-10 minutes, until flesh has become opaque and shells have turned orange.

◆ Serve freshly grilled lobster with discs of herb butter.

Tiger Prawns with Coriander Mayonnaise

SERVES 2

115ML (4FL OZ) SWEET CHILLI SAUCE

4 TABLESPOONS TOMATO PURÉE

4 TEASPOONS LEMON JUICE

4 GARLIC CLOVES, CRUSHED

4 TEASPOONS SESAME OIL

16 RAW UNPEELED TIGER PRAWNS

CORIANDER MAYONNAISE

85G (3FL OZ) MAYONNAISE

½ FRESH RED CHILLI, SEEDED AND FINELY CHOPPED

½ SMALL RED ONION, FINELY CHOPPED

2 TABLESPOONS CHOPPED CORIANDER

2 TABLESPOONS LEMON JUICE

◆ To make marinade, combine sweet chilli sauce, tomato purée, lemon juice, garlic and sesame oil in a large bowl.

◆ Add prawns to bowl of marinade and toss to coat evenly. Cover and refrigerate for 2 hours, if time permits.

◆ To make coriander mayonnaise, mix together mayonnaise, chilli, onion, coriander and lemon juice. Season to taste with salt and pepper. Cover and refrigerate until required.

◆ Thread 4 prawns onto each skewer and cook on a prepared barbecue for 4-5 minutes on each side, turning them once.

◆ Serve prawns hot, on or off skewers, with coriander mayonnaise.

Prawns with Saffron Mayonnaise

SERVES 4

3 TABLESPOONS OLIVE OIL

JUICE 1/2 LEMON

2 GARLIC CLOVES, CRUSHED

1 TABLESPOON CHOPPED FRESH FENNEL

SALT AND FRESHLY GROUND BLACK PEPPER

20 LARGE RAW PRAWNS, HEADS REMOVED

RADICCHIO LEAVES AND FENNEL SPRIGS, TO GARNISH (OPTIONAL)

SAFFRON MAYONNAISE

150ML (5FL OZ) FISH STOCK

GENEROUS PINCH SAFFRON THREADS

150ML (5FL OZ) MAYONNAISE

1 TEASPOON LEMON JUICE

◆ To make marinade, mix together oil, lemon juice, garlic, fennel, salt and pepper.

◆ Put prawns in a shallow dish and pour marinade over. Turn to coat and leave in a cool place for 2 hours.

◆ To make saffron mayonnaise, put fish stock in a saucepan and boil until reduced to 1 tablespoon. Add saffron threads and leave to cool.

◆ Strain stock into a bowl and stir in mayonnaise. Stir in lemon juice, salt and pepper.

◆ Remove prawns from marinade and thread onto skewers. Cook on a prepared barbecue for about 10 minutes, turning once.

◆ Remove prawns from skewers and arrange on serving plates. Garnish with radicchio leaves and fennel, if desired, and serve with saffron mayonnaise.

Prawns with Mango Salsa

SERVES 4

1 FRESH RED CHILLI, SEEDED AND FINELY CHOPPED

½ TEASPOON PAPRIKA

½ TEASPOON GROUND CORIANDER

1 GARLIC CLOVE, CRUSHED

JUICE ½ LIME

2 TABLESPOONS OIL

SALT AND FRESHLY GROUND BLACK PEPPER

20 LARGE RAW UNPEELED PRAWNS

MANGO SALSA

1 MANGO, PEELED AND DICED

½ SMALL RED ONION, FINELY DICED

1 FRESH RED CHILLI, SEEDED AND FINELY CHOPPED

3 TABLESPOONS CHOPPED FRESH CORIANDER

GRATED ZEST AND JUICE 1 LIME

SALT AND FRESHLY GROUND BLACK PEPPER

◆ To make salsa, in a bowl mix together mango, red onion, chilli, coriander, lime zest and juice and salt and pepper. Set aside.

◆ In a bowl, mix together chilli, paprika, coriander, garlic, lime juice, oil and salt and pepper.

◆ Remove dark veins and heads from prawns and discard. Place prawns in a dish, add spice mixture and mix to coat thoroughly. Cover and leave in a cool place for 30 minutes.

◆ Thread prawns onto skewers and cook on a prepared barbecue for 6-8 minutes until pink, basting and turning frequently.

◆ Serve prawns with mango salsa.

Prawns with Asian-style Sauce

SERVES 4-6

Handful Thai or ordinary fresh basil, finely chopped

2 tablespoons finely chopped garlic

2 tablespoons finely chopped fresh ginger

2 tablespoons finely chopped fresh green chillies

2 teaspoons rice wine or medium dry sherry

2½ tablespoons groundnut oil

1 teaspoon Chinese sesame oil

Salt and pepper

700g (1½lb) large raw prawns

Lime wedges and basil sprigs, to garnish

◆ To make marinade, pound together basil, garlic, ginger, chillies, rice wine or sherry, groundnut and sesame oils and seasoning using a pestle and mortar.

◆ Remove legs and heads from prawns and discard. Using strong scissors, cut prawns lengthways in half leaving tails intact. Remove dark veins.

◆ Rub marinade over prawns and place in a bowl. Cover and leave in a cool place for 1 hour.

◆ Cook prawns in a single layer on a prepared barbecue for about 3 minutes until curled, or 'butterflied', and bright pink.

◆ Garnish with lime wedges and basil sprigs. Serve any remaining marinade separately.

Prawns with Sun-dried Tomato and Basil Dip

SERVES 4

450G (1LB) LARGE RAW PRAWNS

JUICE 1 LEMON

5 TABLESPOONS EXTRA VIRGIN OLIVE OIL

½ GARLIC CLOVE, CRUSHED

2 TABLESPOONS SUN-DRIED TOMATO PASTE

PINCH CAYENNE

1 TABLESPOON CHOPPED FRESH BASIL

SALT AND FRESHLY GROUND BLACK PEPPER

FRESH BASIL LEAVES, TO GARNISH

◆ Remove head and legs from prawns. Using sharp scissors cut prawns lengthways almost in half, leaving tail end intact.

◆ Place prawns in a shallow dish and pour over half the lemon juice and 2 tablespoons olive oil. Stir in garlic. Leave for at least 30 minutes.

◆ Remove prawns from marinade and arrange in a single layer on the barbecue rack. Cook over hot coals for about 3 minutes until prawns have curled or 'butterflied' and are bright pink.

◆ In a small bowl, mix together remaining lemon juice and 3 tablespoons olive oil, sun-dried tomato paste, cayenne, basil and salt and pepper.

◆ Either spoon sauce over prawns or serve separately for dipping. Garnish prawns with basil sprigs.

Stuffed Squid with Sesame and Cashew Nuts

12 PREPARED BABY SQUID TUBES

2 TABLESPOONS CORNFLOUR, SIFTED

2 EGG WHITES, BEATEN

2 TEASPOONS LIGHT SOY SAUCE

1 TEASPOON SESAME OIL

175G (6OZ) RAW CASHEW NUTS, FINELY CHOPPED

4 TABLESPOONS SESAME SEEDS

THAI SWEET CHILLI SAUCE, TO SERVE

SHREDDED SPRING ONION AND CUCUMBER, TO SERVE

STUFFING

350G (12OZ) COOKED WHITE RICE

4 SPRING ONIONS, FINELY CHOPPED

2 TEASPOONS FINELY CHOPPED FRESH GINGER

1 TEASPOON FINELY CHOPPED FRESH RED CHILLI

2 TEASPOONS LIGHT SOY SAUCE

◆ To make stuffing, place cooked rice, spring onions, ginger, chilli and soy sauce in a food processor and blend briefly until well combined. Stuff cavities of squid with rice mixture.

◆ In a small bowl, mix together cornflour, egg whites, soy sauce and sesame oil.

◆ Mix cashew nuts and sesame seeds together and spread out on a plate.

◆ Dip each stuffed squid tube in egg mixture and then roll in cashew nut mixture to coat evenly.

◆ Secure the end of each squid tube with a cocktail stick to hold in stuffing. Chill coated squid in refrigerator for 2 hours.

◆ Oil a griddle plate and heat it on a prepared barbecue. Cook squid on griddle for about 8 minutes, turning occasionally until golden.

◆ Serve squid hot with chilli sauce and shredded spring onion and cucumber.

Angels on Horseback

SERVES 4 AS A STARTER

4 BACON SLICES, RINDS REMOVED

8 SHELLED OYSTERS

4 SLICES BREAD

UNSALTED BUTTER FOR SPREADING

FRESHLY GROUND BLACK PEPPER

LAMB'S LETTUCE AND LEMON TWISTS, TO GARNISH

◆ Cut each bacon slice crossways in half, then stretch each piece.

◆ Wrap a piece of bacon around each oyster and place on the rack of a prepared barbecue, tucking ends of bacon underneath. Cook until just crisp on both sides.

◆ Toast bread, then cut 2 circles from each slice of toast using a pastry cutter. Butter circles.

◆ Place an oyster on each toast circle, grind over black pepper and serve garnished with lamb's lettuce and lemon twists.

Prawn Paste on Sugar Cane

SERVES 4-6 AS A STARTER

400G (14OZ) RAW PEELED PRAWNS

55G (2OZ) FRESH FATTY PORK, CHOPPED

1/2 TEASPOON CHOPPED GARLIC

SALT AND FRESHLY GROUND BLACK PEPPER

1 TEASPOON SUGAR

1 TABLESPOON CORNFLOUR

1 EGG WHITE, BEATEN

30CM (12IN) PIECE SUGAR CANE

CORIANDER SPRIGS, TO GARNISH

SPICY FISH SAUCE (SEE PAGE 59), TO SERVE

◆ Using a pestle and mortar, pound prawns, pork and garlic to a smooth paste. Place in a bowl and add salt, pepper, sugar, cornflour and beaten egg white. Mix to blend well.

◆ Peel sugar cane, cut into 3 equal pieces and split lengthways into 4.

◆ Mould prawn paste onto sugar cane, leaving about 2.5cm (1in) of sugar cane at one end uncovered, to use as a handle.

◆ Place sticks on rack over medium-hot coals and cook for 5-6 minutes, turning to ensure even cooking.

◆ Garnish with coriander sprigs and serve with a bowl of spicy fish sauce.

Note: Once prawn paste is eaten, sugar cane can be sucked and chewed.

Prawns with Ginger Dip

SERVES 4

16 LARGE RAW PRAWNS, PEELED BUT WITH
TAILS LEFT ON

1 TABLESPOON LIGHT SOY SAUCE

1 TEASPOON RICE WINE

1 TEASPOON SESAME OIL

1 GARLIC CLOVE, CRUSHED

CORIANDER LEAVES AND GINGER STRIPS,
TO GARNISH

GINGER DIP

1 TABLESPOON WHITE RICE VINEGAR

1 TEASPOON SUGAR

2 TABLESPOONS CHOPPED FRESH
CORIANDER

1CM (½IN) PIECE FRESH GINGER,
PEELED AND FINELY CHOPPED

◆ Using a small sharp knife, cut along back of each prawn and remove and discard thin black vein. Rinse and dry prawns with absorbent kitchen paper and place on a plate.

◆ To make marinade, mix together soy sauce, rice wine, sesame oil and garlic in a small bowl. Brush over prawns. Cover and chill for 1 hour.

◆ To make dip, mix together rice vinegar, sugar, coriander and ginger in a small bowl. Cover and chill until required.

◆ Place prawns on a barbecue rack and cook for 1-2 minutes on each side, basting with marinade, until bright pink.

◆ Garnish prawns with coriander leaves and ginger strips and serve with ginger dip.

Squid with Aubergine and Rocket

SERVES 4

2 GARLIC CLOVES, FINELY CHOPPED

2 TABLESPOONS OLIVE OIL

JUICE 1 LEMON

1 TEASPOON SWEET CHILLI SAUCE

2 SMALL RED CHILLIES, SEEDED AND CHOPPED

700G (1½LB) BABY SQUID, CLEANED, TUBES AND TENTACLES SEPARATED

VEGETABLE OIL FOR BRUSHING

2 MEDIUM AUBERGINES, VERY THINLY SLICED

115G (4OZ) ROCKET

LEMON WEDGES, TO SERVE

◆ In a bowl mix together garlic, olive oil, lemon juice, chilli sauce and chillies. Stir squid into marinade, cover and leave in a cool place to marinate for 2 hours.

◆ Heat a griddle on a prepared barbecue until smoking and brush with oil. Grill aubergine slices in batches for 2 minutes on each side. Transfer to a warm oven to keep warm.

◆ Remove squid from marinade and reserve marinade. Heat griddle until searing hot and fry squid for about 20 seconds on each side, then transfer to a plate.

◆ Pour marinade into a small saucepan and heat gently.

◆ Arrange aubergine slices on 4 warmed plates. Pile squid on top and spoon over a little marinade. Surround each portion with a ring of rocket leaves. Serve at once, with lemon wedges.

Index